THE AUTHORS

NIGEL WEBB is Chairman of the Dorset Wildlife Trust, which he joined forty years ago. Born and educated in Bristol, he read zoology at the University of Wales followed by post-graduate research. He joined the staff of Furzebrook Research Station in 1967 and retired as Deputy Head of the Station in 2002. An internationally known ecologist, and author of the New Naturalist volume on heathlands, he is an authority on European heathlands, tundra, conservation biology, and restoration ecology. He has served on the Council of the British Ecological Society, as Editor of the *Journal of Applied Ecology*, and as a Vice President of the Institute of Biology.

TONY BATES is President of the Dorset Wildlife Trust, which he joined in the early 1970s. He was brought up in Devon and Yorkshire and obtained a degree in Materials Science at the University of Wales. He worked for major engineering companies in both the Midlands and Australia, where photography was an important aspect of his role. His career then brought him to Dorset to work at the Winfrith Technology Centre. He became a Council member of the Dorset Wildlife Trust in the early 1990s and was appointed Chairman in 1998, the position he held until 2010. From 2000 until 2006 he served as a Council member of the Royal Society of Wildlife Trusts.

FOLLOWING PAGES
Cowslips in spring on Melbury Down.

THE DOVECOTE PRESS

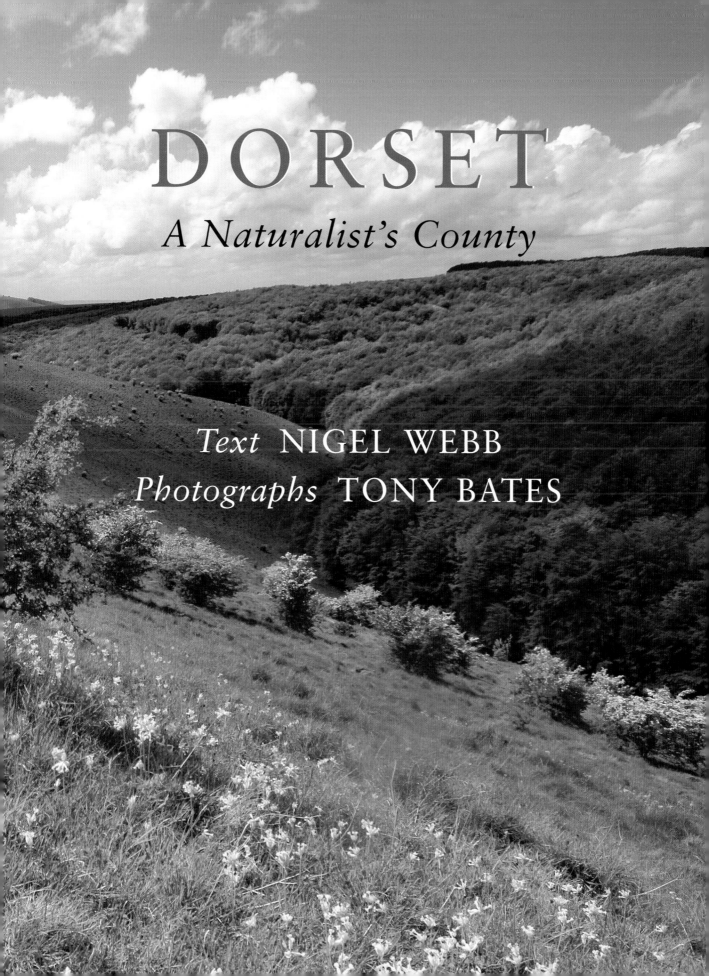

DORSET
A Naturalist's County

Text NIGEL WEBB
Photographs TONY BATES

This book is dedicated to the memory of Helen Brotherton and all those who helped in the founding of the Dorset Wildlife Trust.

Chalkhill blue butterfly on Fontmell Down.

First published in 2011 by The Dovecote Press Ltd
Stanbridge, Wimborne Minster, Dorset BH21 4JD

ISBN 978-1-904-34993-8
Text © Nigel Webb 2011
Photographs © Tony Bates 2011 (also see Acknowledgements)

Nigel Webb has asserted his rights under the Copyright, Designs and Patent Act 1988 to be identified as author of this work

Designed by The Dovecote Press
Printed and bound in Spain by GraphyCems, Navarra

All papers used by The Dovecote Press are natural, recyclable products made from wood grown in sustainable, well-managed forests

A CIP catalogue record for this book is available from the British Library

Contents

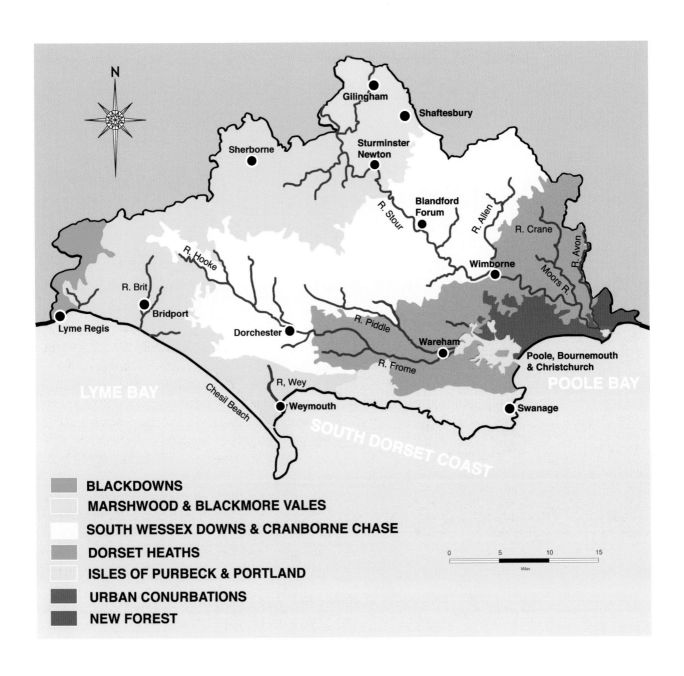

N

Gilingham

Shaftesbury

Sherborne

Sturminster
Newton

Blandford
Forum

R. Allen

R. Crane

R. Avon

R. Stour

Wimborne

Moors R.

R. Hooke

R. Brit

Bridport

Dorchester

R. Piddle

Wareham

Lyme Regis

Poole, Bournemouth
& Christchurch

R. Frome

LYME BAY

Chesil Beach

R, Wey

Weymouth

POOLE BAY

Swanage

SOUTH DORSET COAST

BLACKDOWNS
MARSHWOOD & BLACKMORE VALES
SOUTH WESSEX DOWNS & CRANBORNE CHASE
DORSET HEATHS
ISLES OF PURBECK & PORTLAND
URBAN CONURBATIONS
NEW FOREST

0   5   10   15
Miles

Foreword

SIR DAVID ATTENBOROUGH OM, CH, CVO, CBE, FRS

Sir David Attenborough and Helen Brotherton in 1992, when Helen Brotherton was awarded the Christopher Cadbury Medal in recognition of the outstanding contribution she made to the advancement of nature conservation in the British Isles.

Since the twenty-fifth anniversary of the Dorset Wildlife Trust in 1986 there have been immense changes to the way in which the environment is perceived. One example is that in addition to increasing its portfolio of nature reserves the Trust now guides and advises landowners on the importance of management of land for wildlife on over 1000 sites throughout the county as part of its vision of the 'Living Landscape'.

Increasingly the Trust works to engage with the local community through 5 wildlife centres in the rural, marine and urban environment. It could not do this without many dedicated volunteers that work together with the staff, and the support of over 25,000 members. I am very aware of the ever increasing pressure on our wildlife and I know that the Trust will play a valuable part in helping create a better environment for us all in the twenty-first century.

The Dorset Wildlife Trust has now produced this book - *Dorset, A Naturalist's County*, to help mark the celebrations of its fiftieth anniversary this year. I am sure you will enjoy it. It traces the growth of a concern for Dorset's rich natural history, beginning with the pioneering work of the early nineteenth century county naturalists, right through to the start of the Wildlife Trust movement and to the work it is doing today to save and protect the natural world on which we all depend.

Introduction

'*The County of Dorset is small, but yet so varied in its configuration as to present an epitome of the scenery of southern England*'.
SIR FREDERICK TREVES
Highways and Byways in Dorset (1906)

Treves was not exaggerating; within an area of about 1000 square miles you will find in Dorset one of the most diverse and attractive landscapes in the whole of Britain. The exceptional variety of plants and animals that can be found in the county has long been recognized; it has drawn naturalists to Dorset for at least three centuries. The patchwork of undulating thickly hedged meadows in Dorset's western vales are rich in flowers. As recently as 2002, the 10km Ordnance Survey grid square encompassing Wareham and Corfe Castle, in the north of the Isle of Purbeck, was widely publicised as containing the greatest number of species of vascular plants compared with any other similar square in the British Isles.

The richness does not stop there; it is to be found in many other groups of plants and animals. There are some 48 species of butterfly within the county with a further six species which have become extinct. Twenty eight of the 39 species of dragon and damsel fly found in Britain breed in the county; thirty three of the 36 species of grasshoppers and crickets are to be found in Dorset; all six species of British reptile

Lewesdon Hill and the Marshwood Vale from Pilsdon Pen.

9

OPPOSITE PAGE AND ABOVE Such is Dorset's variety that it can range from the heaths on the western edge of Poole Harbour to the wooded valleys at Kingcombe near Powerstock and the fossil-rich coast at Lyme Regis. RIGHT Two rare heathland species. The ruddy darter dragonfly and a large marsh grasshopper.

occur here; more spiders have been recorded here than in any similar area in Britain. The list is endless; Dorset is probably one the most bio-diverse regions in Britain, and we would not be wrong in calling it a 'biodiversity hot spot'.

Recently, the richness of the coastline has been recognised by the designation Jurassic Coast – a UNESCO World Heritage Site; a protected coastline of 95 miles made up of rocks spaning 185 million years of the earth's history. This coastline is of unsurpassed scenery and geological interest. A number of places in Dorset are known to geologists the world over in the naming of geological strata: – the Purbeck and Portland Beds, Kimmeridge Clays and the Black

Two views of the heath. Hardown Hill and winter on Black Hill, near Bere Regis.

Dorset's coast is as varied as its rural landscapes.
TOP The undercliff at the chalk headland of White Nothe.
MIDDLE Purbeck limestone at the western side of the
Stairhole at Lulworth Cove.
BOTTOM East Cliff, West Bay, showing the Bridport
Sandstone from the Upper Lias zone of the Jurrasic Coast.

Ven Marls. It is not surprising that geology students have for years come to Dorset for their field work.

Inland, considerable areas of the county are designated as Areas of Outstanding Beauty. There are a large number of nature reserves, either National Nature Reserves or reserves held by conservation bodies. The Dorset Wildlife Trust has itself 42 nature reserves. These are supported by a substantial network of Sites of Special Scientific Interest and other conservation designations. Extensive areas of land, especially on the coast, are owned and managed by the National Trust. In many case these various conservation designations overlap and there are few areas within the county which do not fall under one designation or another.

Why is Dorset so rich? The topographic and biological diversity of the county stems from the rich variety of the underlying rocks, which is unequalled almost anywhere else in the British Isles. Like Britain as a whole, the youngest strata are to be found in the east of the county and the oldest in the west. This variety of rocks in turn produces a variety of soils.

Acting on top of all of this is the climate. The climate of Dorset is intermediate between the more continental climate of the south-east of England and the oceanic south-west. There is a marked gradient across the county from east to west and in turn this combined with the soils and varying topography account for the county's rich biodiversity.

For the most part, the county consists of many small villages together with market towns such as Dorchester, Blandford Forum, Sturminster Newton, Gillingham, Sherborne and Wareham.

ABOVE The green zone that borders the sea shore provides a valuable wildlife habitat close to the centre of Bournemouth.

BELOW Kinson Common provides an attractive open space in the midst of a residential area.

Seaside towns such as Swanage, Weymouth, West Bay, Charmouth and Lyme Regis lie along the length of its coast. The east of the county is dominated by the large urban areas of Poole, Bournemouth and Christchurch.

Human activity also plays its part. Within the county boundary there is a microcosm of the principal factors affecting wildlife today. Farming, urban expansion, mineral and oil extraction, tourism and recreation, and military training can all be found. Often these occur close to one another, as for instance around

BELOW LEFT Recent urban development on the fringe of Canford Heath.

BELOW Military training ground on Povington Heath.

ABOVE Looking west from the Valley of Stones towards Little Bredy, almost the western limit of the chalk.

BELOW The River Piddle at Turner's Puddle. The Piddle rises on the downland and flows into Poole Harbour.

Poole Harbour. Again, Dorset is the epitome of southern England with all the problems of maintaining human activity while at the same time finding space for wildlife and maintaining the landscape.

Fifty years ago a determined and dedicated group of naturalists had the vision to see that without action to resist and maintain a balance between people and wildlife the riches of the county would not be available to future generations. Although naturalists were well catered for by local natural history societies, which promoted scientific natural history, these societies were not in a position to go out and protect – or as they preferred to say conserve, plants and animals.

The intervening years have seen great advances. The Dorset Naturalists' Trust was formed in March 1961 with just over 300 members. Before long it had acquired nature reserves and begun influencing policy and planning. Today, as the Dorset Wildlife Trust, it stands as a colossal memorial to its founders as an organisation with some 25,000 members, a staff of over 80 professional conservationists and a nature reserve estate of 1300 hectares. It is a highly influential organisation representing the views of a substantial body of people throughout the county.

The story of the Trust is at the heart of this book. Yet it is a story which needs context, the context of a rich and diverse county, a history of

Beech woodland near Affpuddle in autumn.

active and prominent naturalists set against the evolving background of the ideas and philosophy of wildlife conservation.

This is very much a personal account. I have known Dorset since my childhood, and have lived in it for the last 45 years. This personal viewpoint reflects that of a professional ecologist engaged in conservation research and contains fragments which represent this lifetime. Not only does it set the scene by introducing the county and its naturalists, but dips into ecological

The Lagoon on Brownsea Island nature reserve is an exceptional area for many visiting and nesting waders and wildfowl.

science, the philosophy of nature conservation and the history of conservation in general: topics which have taken my interest and which seem to be relevant to our story. Despite all this, my principal aim is to celebrate fifty years of nature conservation in Dorset.

The Lie of the Land

We have already mentioned that the great variety of species of plants and animals which occur in the county is due to its underlying rocks and the soils formed from them, the climate, the shape of the land, and the ways in which we use it. All these factors interact to create the habitats suitable for plants and animals.

Ecologists define the habitat of a species as the location which provides the right combination of factors and resources, such as food and living space, which each species requires. Habitats must therefore always be defined in relation to a particular named species. However, conservationists often speak loosely of habitats such as heathland, chalk grassland or saltmarsh. This is a misuse of the word as it does not relate to a species but to an assemblage of species. The correct, but less used term, is biotope. For instance, a heathland we recognize as a particular assemblage of species of plants and animals living together under a particular set of conditions. This is a biotope, or to some ecologists an ecosystem. Within the heathland biotope we find the habitats of the individual heathland species, such as the sand lizard or silver-studded blue butterfly.

The habitats of each species result from the interaction of many factors. Some of these are physical, such as soils and climate, while others are biotic, made up by the interactions with other species. These species may be competitors

The Blackmore Vale from Hambledon Hill.

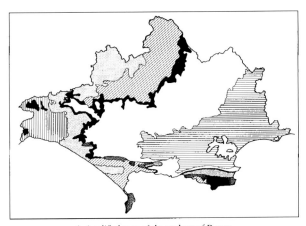

A simplified map of the geology of Dorset.

Tertiary rocks (clays, sands & gravels).

Chalk (limestone).

Lower Greensand, Gault & Upper Greensand (clays & sands).

Wealden (clays, silts, sands & grits).

Portland Sand & Stone & Purbeck Limestone Group (limestones & clays).

Kellaways Beds, Oxford Clay, Corallian & Kimmeridge Clay (limestones & clays).

Inferior Oolite, Fuller's Earth, Frome Clay, Forest Marble & Cornbrash (limestone & clays).

Lower, Middle & Upper Lias (thin limestones, clays, silts & sands).

Two species typically associated with Dorset heathland.
LEFT Male sand lizard in spring colour.
BELOW LEFT Silver-studded blue butterfly.

or they may be food (prey), or predators, or pathogens. It is because there is so great an interaction between these factors that the county is so rich in species.

The landscape of Dorset is dominated by the central outcrop of chalk and other Cretaceous deposits which run across the county from the south-west to the north-east. To the east of the chalk lie younger deposits from the Tertiary. These are really the westernmost extension of what geologists call the Hampshire Basin. This western portion of the Basin is sometimes called the Poole Basin. To the north and west of the chalk escarpment lies a succession of older Jurassic and Liassic rocks sometimes exhibiting strata of great complexity. The geology of Dorset represents on a small scale a division which runs through the south of Britain as a whole. The west of Britain is formed from rocks of the Palaeozoic and older periods. To the east lie younger strata of rocks: Dorset straddles this line.

The central chalk escarpment is a south-westward extension of the large area of chalk which lies beneath Salisbury Plain. The area of chalk is widest where it enters the county high on Cranborne Chase and gradually tapers south-westwards until north of Abbotsbury. From here the chalk divides with one branch running to the north-west towards Beaminister and the Somerset border. The other runs eastwards as a thin outcrop parallel to the coast from Arish Mell and Worbarrow Bay and then as a thin ridge or hogsback through Purbeck to Swanage. It terminates on Ballard Down and the Foreland (Old Harry Rock). Formerly, this ridge was continuous with the chalk on the Isle of Wight and was joined to the Needles.

The chalk escarpment is marked by the vantage points of Melbury Hill, Fontmell Down,

The Foreland and Old Harry mark the eastern end on the chalk and were once joined to the Isle of Wight.

Hambledon Hill, Bulbarrow, Batcombe Hill, Melbury Bubb, Black Down and Eggardon. All of these places reach 200 to 275 metres above sea level and provide stunning views over the landscape of the Vales which make up the north and west of Dorset. In Purbeck the highest point on the chalk is Nine Barrow Down. The great area of chalk occupies almost half the area of the county and is, therefore, of great ecological significance. It is made the more so by the over laying deposits – the so-called clay with flints – which add variety to these soils resulting in a more diverse range of plants.

The rolling chalk downland high on Cranborne Chase.

ABOVE Tadnoll Heath is a typical area of Dorset heathland that developed on the Bagshot Sands.
LEFT The adder, here showing its zig-zag markings, is most common in Dorset on the sandy heath.

To the east the chalk dips slowly and forms a basin – the Poole Basin – which is overlain with deposits of clays, sands and gravels from Tertiary times. These deposits commence as far east as Warmwell and Higher Woodford near Dorchester. In the south the Tertiary deposits run parallel with the chalk ridge of Purbeck to Studland. North-eastwards the boundary of the Tertiary encompasses Bloxworth and proceeds towards Wimborne and Cranborne, and an eastern boundary with the valley of the River Avon. Similar Tertiary deposits occur to the east of the River Avon (the Hampshire Basin) and it is on these that the heathlands of the New Forest have developed.

The Tertiary deposits of Dorset are almost entirely Bagshot Sands, with seams of clay and varying amounts of plateau gravels. It is on the soils derived from these strata that the Dorset heathlands have developed. The rivers which traverse the heathlands are bounded by alluvial deposits and valley gravels. Poole Harbour itself, which forms the lowest point of the Basin, was

formed after the last Ice Age about 6000 years ago when the melting ice caused the sea level to rise and flooded the lowest portion of the Tertiary Basin. One can see that the islands of Poole Harbour are in fact similar to the knolls which outcrop on the surrounding heathlands.

To the north and the west of the chalk escarpment lie the Great Vales; the Marshwood and Blackmore Vales and a number of lesser vales. A complex series of rock strata, which includes Greensand, Gault, Kimmeridge Clay, Corallian Limestone and Oxford Clays, lies to the north-west of the chalk and makes up the

Blackmore Vale. The outermost boundary of these deposits consists of Oolites, Cornbrash with Forest Marbles and Fuller's Earth. The Marshwood and its associated vales in the west have further outcrops of Greensands and Gault, Oolites and Cornbrash. Further west still is a series of Liassic deposits as we move towards the Blackdown Hills of Somerset.

In the south, west of Weymouth, we find Greensands, Gault, Corallian Limestones and

A fossilised tree from Portland limestone in King Barrow Quarry.

Bands of limestone within the shale can be seen at Kimmeridge Bay.

Oxford Clay. The Isle of Portland, itself, is, of course, Portland Limestone, long known as a fine building stone. Further east in Purbeck the chalk is bounded by narrow bands of Greensand and Gault and a wider band of Wealden Clays. To the south of the Purbeck chalk ridge lies a parallel, narrow ridge of Portland and Purbeck Limestones with outcrops of Kimmeridge Clay on the coast.

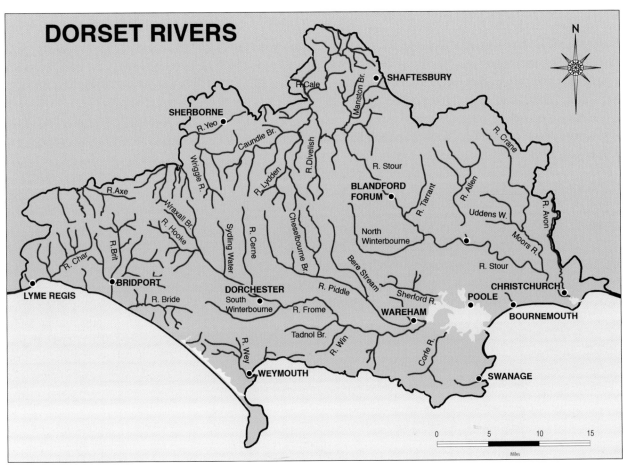

DORSET RIVERS

Thus, from the young and relatively simple variety of rocks and deposits in the east of the county we rise up onto the chalk escarpment. As we drop away sharply into the vales the rock strata become increasingly varied and complex.

Despite the increasing complexity as we move westwards in the county, we can reduce it to a small number of ecological zones based on the river systems and the underlying rocks (see the Map on page 6). The first to do this was Professor Ronald Good in his *Geographical Handbook of the Dorset Flora* (1948).

The chalklands are conveniently divided by the rivers Stour and Frome and their tributaries into the Northern Chalk, the Central Chalk, the Southern Chalk. The clay vales of the north-west and west form further well defined areas. Similarly, the heathlands of the east of the county

Water crowfoot in flower on the Bere Stream, a typical sight in summer on Dorset's chalk streams.

and the Isles of Purbeck and Portland are also well defined units.

Besides the two major rivers, the Frome and the Stour, there is a third, the Piddle. All three drain south-eastwards, with the Frome and Piddle discharging into Poole Harbour, and the Stour into Christchurch Harbour, together with the Hampshire Avon. The rivers Frome and Piddle are classic chalk rivers. They rise on the chalklands where the rainfall percolates through the soil into the underlying porous rock. The water is stored in this rock – the aquifer – and emerges as springs. The aquifer is topped up by rainfall, mainly during the winter months, and discharges its water throughout the year, the

ABOVE The North Winterborne at Winterborne Zelston.
LEFT Dorset's watercress beds owe their success to the
purity and even temperature of the water.
BELOW LEFT The River Allen near Witchampton.

flow rate declining as summer progresses. The release of this water from the aquifer is relatively steady and the water maintains a fairly constant temperature throughout the year of about 11 degrees Celsius. This is an important factor for aquatic organisms. The filtration of the water through the chalk rock results in particularly clear water of a stable chemical composition. The Frome and Piddle are fed by other smaller streams and rivers and as they flow eastward both cross the acidic Tertiary deposits of the heathlands.

While most chalk rivers flow all the year round some only flow in the winter months when the heavier rainfall causes the level of the aquifer to rise in the rock and for springs to emerge. These seasonal rivers or winterbournes are a feature of the chalk and in Dorset there are two main winterbournes: the North Winterbourne which rises above Winterborne Stickland and flows through a series of villages named after the river

until it joins the River Stour near Sturminster Marshall. The South Winterborne rises to the west of Dorchester, flowing to the south of the town through another series of villages named Winterborne before it joins the River Frome near West Stafford.

The River Stour is more complex, rising at Stourhead in Wiltshire from Jurassic deposits then passing through the clay vales of north Dorset where there are numerous tributaries that include the Lodden, Cale and Lydden. It then continues through the chalk to be joined by another chalk stream, the River Allen at Wimborne, before crossing the Tertiary deposits to reach Christchurch Harbour. Of particular significance for wildlife is the River Crane, which begins life on the chalk near Cranborne but, turns into the Moors River when it reaches the heathlands. This combination of alkaline and acidic water creates considerable biological richness.

It is fortunate that the flood plains of the Frome, Piddle and Stour remain largely intact with the exception of parts of the lower reaches of the Stour. Often during the winter months they perform their function as true flood plains and this is significant for the diversity of wildlife

ABOVE The River Stour at Fiddleford Mill.
BELOW The acidic Moors River begins life as the alkaline River Crane, adding greatly to its wildlife.

along these rivers.

The complex rock formations of the west of the county produce rivers of a different quality. The Rivers Axe and Yeo rise in the north-west of the county but both flow westwards into Devon. In the south-west, the Rivers Brit and Char arise within the county and flow through Bridport and Charmouth respectively. To the west of Dorchester the River Bride flows westwards,

The River Hooke at Lower Kingcombe.

discharging into the sea at Burton Bradstock. Several small streams discharge into the Fleet and Weymouth Bay with the River Wey emptying into Radipole Lake. In Purbeck, the Corfe River rises on the Wealden Clays and passes through the chalk ridge and heathlands before entering Poole Harbour. The Sherford River also rises on the chalk, but is relatively short and enters Poole Harbour in Lytchett Bay.

The area of woodland in Dorset is modest compared with many neighbouring counties. Following the last Ice Age woodland would have developed over most of the county in succession to tundra communities and birch woodland. These woodlands would have been mainly of oak, ash, elm and lime together with a range of understory species. However, the light soils of the chalk and the east of the county were easy to clear and the woodland was replaced by a more open landscape as early farming developed. On the chalk in Celtic times this resulted in considerable soil erosion, creating even thinner soils.

Nevertheless, the area of woodland in Dorset has fluctuated over the centuries. It was probably least in the early nineteenth century – a period before which timber was in great demand for shipbuilding. Since then the acreage has steadily increased, although not necessarily of typical traditional species. Thomas Hardy remarks in the introduction to *The Return of the Native* of how the open heathlands – his Egdon Heath – 'is disguised by intrusive strips and slices brought under the plough with varying degrees of success, or planted to woodland'.

Nevertheless, despite the increased planting, less than 10% of Dorset is woodland today. Fine woods still exist, such as Duncliffe Wood, Piddles Wood, Oakers Wood, Chetterwood, Creech Great Wood, Powerstock, Melbury, Edmonsham and the woodlands on Cranborne Chase. Many of these can be termed 'ancient', that is to say they have been woodland for many centuries; however, we must remember that they have been affected by human activity throughout. Timber, underwood and brush, as well as other materials, will have long been harvested from them, yet the

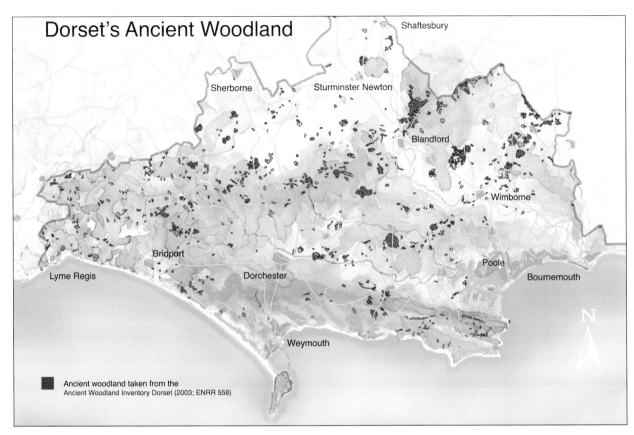

Dorset's Ancient Woodland

Shaftesbury

Sherborne

Sturminster Newton

Blandford

Wimborne

Bridport

Poole

Lyme Regis

Dorchester

Bournemouth

Weymouth

N

▪ Ancient woodland taken from the
Ancient Woodland Inventory Dorset (2003; ENRR 558)

RIGHT The Dorset Wildlife Trust Nature Reserve at
Hibbits Woods. Moss covered fallen wood and red elf cup
fungi in early spring.

woodlands have renewed themselves.

An important element in such woodland has been coppicing. Trees for timber were grown to produce tall un-branched trunks. Where poles and smaller timber was required, trees were cut young and allowed to re-sprout, producing a continuous supply. Many areas of former coppice can be seen throughout the county, although much has now grown out. The more open conditions in the early years of the coppice rotation produced a rich ground flora with associated insects, particularly butterflies.

There are other areas in Dorset to which the term forest can be found. These are ancient royal hunting forests, where hunting rather than timber production was the aim. These lands were not necessarily wooded and were subject to

ABOVE Ancient oak tree at Powerstock Common.
LEFT Oakers Wood: one of Dorset's few ancient woodlands, rich in lichens.
BELOW LEFT Wood spurge in hazel coppice at Garston Wood.

Forest Law. Forests such as those at Powerstock, Bere, Holt, Gillingham, Blackmore and Purbeck are examples. Today, some of these have been planted with conifers.

The widespread planting of conifers, rather than broadleaved trees has been characteristic of the twentieth century but began, as Thomas Hardy noted, in the mid nineteenth. Some of the finest areas of open heathland we have today were at this time planted with conifers. A good example is Hartland Moor National Nature Reserve – a very fine area of heathland. This was planted with conifers in the mid nineteenth century and they persisted until the First World War when the last of them was destroyed in a heathland fire. This is an important reminder of how much the landscape has changed over the centuries.

Some of the earliest planting by the then

newly formed Forestry Commission was in what is now known as Wareham Forest in the 1920s. Today, although the extent of woodland in Dorset is greater than it has been in the last two centuries, some two thirds of this area is conifer plantations. This is particularly the case on the acid soils in the east of the county. If the conifers planted on heathland were to be removed the area of heathland would be doubled.

The famous heathlands of Dorset began to develop during the Bronze Age occupation of the area about 3600 years ago. The Bronze Age peoples started clearing the forest, thus encouraging the spread of heathers and scrub. Further clearances about 3000 years ago finally resulted in widespread heathland on these sandy soils. The transition to open heathland was caused by the pastoral activities of these early farmers was well as a change in the climate. This was broadly the picture by the Iron Age and remained so until the mid eighteenth century.

The activities of the farmers involved grazing the heaths, cutting and burning of vegetation, and the cutting of peat and turf. These prevented the regeneration of woodland and ensured that the soils remained depleted of essential plant nutrients. We can gain an impression of the heathland landscape at this time from the

ABOVE Conifer plantation on Rempstone Heath.
BELOW The heath near Arne in about 1890, when it was still being cut for peat and turf.

writings of Thomas Hardy, particularly in *The Return of the Native*.

From the eighteenth century onwards improvements in farming practice resulted in the conversion of heathland to more productive farmland or to forestry. In later years considerable areas of heathland were lost as Poole and Bournemouth expanded.

Much of Dorset is made up of fields, meadows, grasslands, downland and hedgerows. These open areas are the result of human activity over several millennia, during which the original

ABOVE Four of Dorset's dragonflies and damselflies. The small red damselfly (*top left*), common blue damselfly (*top right*), beautiful demoiselle (*bottom left*), and the southern hawker (*bottom right*).

BELOW Winfrith Heath, one of Dorset's finest reserves.

woodland was gradually cleared. The fortunes of these landscapes have changed continuously over the years. The main influences have been the prevailing economic conditions, changing tastes, the Enclosure Acts, a steadily rising population, wars, changes in farming techniques and grazing levels, the use of fertilizers, pesticides, and the development of new varieties of seeds.

The Napoleonic Wars saw a period in which the extent of arable land was, perhaps, the greatest it had ever been, only to decline considerably when cheap cereals were imported from America in the late nineteenth century. It then became uneconomic to grow cereals and the land was abandoned. There have been other times in earlier centuries when land was abandoned such as during the Black Death in the mid fourteenth century. Even in modern times we see changes in the landscape, sometimes from year to year, driven by social and economic factors.

Upton Heath, a valuable area of remaining heath in an urban area now protected from future development.

Occasionally too, biological factors may operate. One of the most pronounced was the disappearance of rabbits in the mid-1950s due to the spread of myxomatosis. The high densities of rabbits suppressed the growth of vegetation, creating smooth, grassy turf. This all changed and the countryside became more lush when the rabbits disappeared. Today, high numbers of deer, wild boar and badgers can induce physical changes in the countryside. It must be remembered, however, that all of these were present in the past and helped shape the landscape.

The presence of wild boar as a factor in the ecology of woodlands is frequently overlooked. In the past they would have been very important, affecting regeneration of the trees and the composition of the ground flora. Today our

33

concept of woodland omits wild boar as an ecological component. What we see today has often been created by ecological processes which no longer operate. We must avoid the tendency to explain what we now see only by the processes operating today.

The past changes in the composition and structure of the landscape and the species it contains raises an important issue for conservation. Our landscape is not natural. It has for millennia been subject to human influence and modification. So, where does the baseline lie? We set our baselines at an arbitrary point, and we judge conservation success as to whether or not a species has increased or declined from this point. In Britain this seems to be the biodiversity created by the agriculture and land uses practices of the mid twentieth century: the period before farming intensified.

However, we set our baselines in a purely arbitrary way. For instance, we mourn the decline in farmland birds as a result of the change from spring-sown to winter sown cereals. Yet we forget that the high populations of these birds were created by the practice of leaving the cereal field fallow over the winter, thus creating a food source for the birds of split grain. If we go back further in time the extent of cereal fields would have been much less, as for instance in the severe agricultural depression of the late nineteenth century. Where were the large populations of seed-eating birds then?

The chalk soils dominate the central part of the county. At first these upland areas were cultivated for crops which resulted in considerable erosion, making it difficult for woodland to re-establish. The chalk downlands became the open landscape we know and were settled from the earliest times. The wealth of ancient earthworks and barrows indicate that these lands were more populated then, despite the lack of water in many places.

Later in the Middle Age sheep pasture

predominated. With the grazing practices there developed a characteristic type of grassland, which was permanent and rich in plant species. At the height of the wool trade in the seventeenth century it has been estimated that there may have been as many as ten million sheep in Dorset.

By the mid eighteenth century the numbers had dwindled to some 800,000. This was still sufficient to suggest a county of downland dominated by sheep, leading John Claridge to write in 1793, 'The most striking feature of the county is the open and unenclosed parts, covered by numerous flocks of sheep, scattered over the Downs, which are in general of a delightful verdure and smoothness affording a scene beautifully picturesque.'

From this time onwards the extent of downland began to decline, a process which accelerated during the late twentieth century as more and more permanent pasture was converted to cereal growing. Although we think of large open arable fields as a modern feature, where in the past there was arable farming on the chalk large, open fields were typical and could be as much as 50-60 acres in extent. This was possible because the light free-draining soils could easily be ploughed by a team of horses.

Today, good examples of species-rich chalk grassland only persist as scattered fragments, often on the steep slopes of the escarpment, which are difficult to cultivate. We find good examples on Melbury Down in the north-east of the county and south-westwards through Hod Hill, Bulbarrow and Bingham's Melcombe to Cerne Abbas, Sydling St Nicholas and Cattistock and onwards to Eggardon and Litton Cheney. There are further areas eastwards at Bincombe, Lulworth and Corfe Castle to Swanage. These steep slopes, especially where they are south

Species-rich neutral pasture land at Kingcombe Meadows Nature Reserve.

facing and warm, are ideal for many plant and insects, especially butterflies.

Many of the species characteristic of these grasslands depend on a short sward for their survival. The rich turf of fine-leaved grasses and rosette forming plants, so characteristic of this community, can contain as many as 40 plant species per square metre. In the past, the key to maintaining the sward was grazing. Where grasslands remain they are often not adequately grazed to maintain the short turf, rich in plant species, which many insects require.

This turf which develops in the more acidic surface layers of the chalk soil is also susceptible to inputs of fertilizer. These additional nutrients, especially nitrogen, encourage the more vigorous species and the sward becomes dominated by tall grasses and the loss of the herbs.

In the clay vales to the north and west of the county we find neutral grasslands often interspersed with more acidic grasslands. These grasslands, which can be rich in plant species and a beautiful sight in the spring and summer, are characteristic of west Dorset, and the Trust's Kingcombe Meadows Reserve contains many fine examples. Another feature of the small scale landscape of the vales, particularly the Marshwood Vale, is the hedgerows.

For the geologist and the fossil collector, the coast of Dorset is exceptional. However, we should not forget that it contains a wealth of plant and animal species. Most of the coast is rocky and the only significant area of sandy beach and dunes is to be found at Studland. The dunes system on the Studland peninsula is unusual because it is formed from acidic and not calcareous sands. The sand which makes up most dune systems in the British Isles is formed from sea shells which are weathered and ground down by the action of the seas. This material is then re-deposited by the wind to form dunes.

At Studland, the acidic Bagshot Sands form the spine of the peninsula. At their southern end these deposits outcrop to the sea and are eroded. The eroded sand is carried by the currents northwards and is re-deposited along the shore. These sands are then blown inland to form the dune ridges. Although the outermost ridges have a flora of maritime plants such as marram grass and sea lyme grass, the inner ridges are clothed in heathland because of the acidic sand.

The processes which formed this dune system were worked out by Cyril Diver, the first Director General of the Nature Conservancy, during his survey of the peninsula in the 1930s. He used old maps of the area to reconstruct the formation of the dunes. In the mid eighteenth century the innermost dune ridge began to form but remained open at its northern end. Gradually this opening closed to cut off the Little Sea, which then became a brackish lagoon. Further dune ridges continued to build over the intervening years: each ridge being about a century younger than the previous one.

Poole Harbour is one of the largest natural harbours in the world. Geologically speaking the Harbour is a recent feature with an origin in Flandrian times when the post-glacial rise in sea level flooded the lowest parts of the Poole Basin. The greatest incursion of the sea was about 6000 years ago and this old shoreline is visible around the Harbour. Since then the sea level has fallen slightly.

The shoreline of the harbour has changed over the centuries, originally by the deposition of sediment carried down by the rivers and in recent times by land reclamation. As a result of these processes, both natural and man-made, the area of the Harbour has reduced by about 1000 hectares over the last six thousand years to its present area of about 3600 hectares. As we have already noted, the rivers Frome and Piddle, together with smaller rivers such as the Sherford Corfe and various streams drain into

the Harbour. The total catchment draining into the Harbour is some 300 square miles.

The Harbour entrance is formed by two low lying sandy spits, at Sandbanks and Studland, thought to have been formed by erosion and longshore drift. Both were formerly heathland, but at Sandbanks extensive development has changed the area while the Studland peninsula remains largely unchanged. The narrow entrance to the Harbour formed by these two spits prevent the transport of marine sediments into the Harbour and the extent to which the body of water changes.

About 80% of the area of the Harbour is intertidal, consisting of sandflats, mudflats, marshes and a system of channels and creeks. The double high water, a feature of this part of the south coast, is particularly important as it reduces the amount of time for which the intertidal areas are available for wading birds to feed. The Harbour has a diverse range of shorelines, ranging from reed and marsh covered mudflats to sandflats and shingle beaches. If we include the dune systems at the Harbour mouth and the chalk cliffs to the south then within this small area almost all the principal types of

The outer dune ridges at Studland.

37

Poole Harbour from Godlingstone Heath.

coastline communities to be found in the British Isles are present.

One of the characteristic and biologically interesting features of Poole Harbour is the saltmarshes dominated by common cord grass (*Spartina anglica*). This is a complicated story. In about 1870 a hybrid arose in Southampton Water between the native *S. maritima* and the North American species *S. alterniflora*, an introduced species. Although this hybrid (known as *S. townsendii*) spread, it was not until it underwent further genetic change to become the new species now called *S. anglica* that it began to form extensive saltmarshes. This new species first appeared in Poole Harbour in about 1890 and had an amazing ability to trap sediment and build up a marsh. It spread rapidly and by 1924 covered some 775 hectares of the tidal mudflats of the Harbour, changing its whole character and structure. However, as the years have passed the extent of these marshes has declined considerably.

Poole Harbour is perhaps best known for its birds. The fringing and extensive reed beds provide the habitat for many species, which in the past included the marsh harrier. However it is the wildfowl and waders for which the Harbour is best known. In winter there are flocks of Brent geese as well as ducks, grebes and divers. Among the many species of wader are nationally important wintering flocks of black-tailed godwit and avocet. There are good populations all year round of shelduck, herons breed on Brownsea Island as well as little egret, and there are extensive colonies of breeding gulls, particularly black-headed, on the saltmarshes near Holton Heath.

The range of habitats in the Harbour is increased by the islands, of which the principal ones are Brownsea, Furzey, Long, Round and Green Island. Brownsea Island, of which we shall hear more later, has heathland, coniferous woodland, reed beds and carr as well as the highly significant lagoon, which is noted for its wildfowl and waders, and colonies of breeding terns. Red squirrels occur both on Furzey Island, where they were introduced, and on Brownsea Island. Furzey Island together with areas on the southern shores of Poole Harbour contains, unobtrusively, the largest onshore oil field in Europe.

Other important wetland areas are to be found around Weymouth, particularly the fine reserves at Lodmoor and Radipole.

The mud and sandflats of Poole Harbour, together with the sandy beaches at Sandbanks,

Bournemouth and Studland lie in east Dorset. It is not until Weymouth that there are further areas of sandy beach, then again not until the far west of the county. For the most part the coastline is rocky.

A significant section of the Dorset coast which is not rocky is Chesil Beach. This unique feature extends from West Bay to Weymouth and forms the link to the mainland for the Isle of Portland. The action of the winds and the tides resulted in a sorting and grading of the pebbles that form this great ridge. The largest are to be found at Portland and they progressively diminish in size westwards to West Bay where they are like small peas.

The eastern section of the beach encloses a brackish lagoon, the Fleet. This stretch of open water extends from Abbottsbury to Portland, where it connects with the sea. However, westwards beyond Abbotsbury there are, in places, extensive marshy areas behind the beach. The beach itself has notable flora which finds a foothold among the pebbles and includes sea pea, yellow-horned poppy and sea kale. Towards the margins of the Fleet the vegetation is richer, with annual seablite, sea spurge, sea sandwort and other salt marsh species.

On one section of the beach is a long-standing colony of little tern. The nest material and

Two views of the Chesil Beach: thrift in flower in early May at the eastern end of the Fleet and sea kale at Cogden Beach to the west.

39

Limestone strata at Clavell's Hard, east of Kimmeridge Bay.

droppings of these birds adds valuable humus and nitrogen to the otherwise hostile pebbles, encouraging a richer vegetation to develop. As the pebble size diminishes to the west the beach becomes more stable and is colonized by a greater range of plants, amongst which are rarities such as sea holly and sea bindweed. The beach is also noted for its invertebrates and is the only site in Britain for the scaly cricket.

The remainder of the Dorset coast consists of the famous cliffs noted for their scenery and beauty. The cliffs represent a wide variety of the principal rock strata to be found in southern Britain. These are mostly sedimentary in origin and were laid down under both marine and freshwater conditions. The oldest strata are from the Triassic period of some 220 million years ago. These form the cliffs at the western end of the county around Lyme Regis and are famous for their fossils.

Next in age are the cliffs formed from the Jurassic period, some 213-144 million years ago. These contain some of the finest and most characteristic rocks for which Dorset is known, Portland limestone, which is widely used as building stone. Elsewhere, there are oolitic limestones and sandstones together with clays and shales; the oil-bearing shales of Kimmeridge being particularly characteristic.

Above the Jurassic strata lie those from the Cretaceous, dating from some 145-65 million years ago. The lowest are the Purbeck limestones, again an important building stone. This is overlain by the Wealden Beds and then the various strata of chalk. These cliffs are high and white and give rise to features such as Old Harry Rock at the eastern end of the Isle of Purbeck.

The different rock strata are subject to erosion, the rate differing from strata to strata. The cliffs in the vicinity of Lyme Regis are noted for their instability, yet this not only reveals the fossils they contain but gives rise to a particular flora and fauna. Similarly, chalk also erodes and here again open conditions are maintained, producing warmer conditions and short vegetation. This creates the habitat of many plant species and insects, particularly butterflies.

The rocky coastline provides an important range of habitats in the intertidal zone. This is colonised by a wide range of seaweeds, as well as a host of intertidal invertebrates, including many species of molluscs, crustaceans, starfish and sea anemones and their relatives. The coastal zone is particularly rich and a wonderful place to study the ecology of the intertidal area.

Recently, it has been possible to survey the sea bed beyond the coastal margin. For the first time we have been able to view the topography of the sea bed, to map the distribution of the various sediments and strata and to have a picture of the distribution of the subtidal flora and fauna.

The final factor that shapes the richness of the flora and fauna of Dorset is its climate. This is very much influenced by its location in the centre of the south coast of England. As we have seen, Dorset straddles a line between the east and the west. So does the climate, which in the east of the county is more continental, with a greater contrast between summer and winter. The west of the county is much more oceanic. It has higher rainfall and more equitable temperatures throughout the year. The movement of rain-bearing depressions from west to east means that the county is wettest in the west and driest in east. Typically some 1100mm per year of rains falls in the west. This rises as we ascend the chalk escarpment to 1300mm. It reduces to less than 900mm in the north and east of the county. There is a similar temperature gradient from west to east. This is modified in the coastal areas by the sea, which has a dampening effect and causes temperature changes to lag behind those further inland. This leads to a longer warm period in autumn and a corresponding lag in the rise of temperature in the spring. The soils also exert an effect, with the sandy soils of the east warming more quickly than the heavier clay soils of the north and west of the county.

There must be few places where in such a small area it is possible to have such a wide variety of rocks, of soils, topography and climatic variation. It is the interaction of these factors which underlies the biological richness of Dorset, making it genuinely a 'biodiversity hotspot'.

BELOW Roe deer.

TWO

Dorset's Naturalists

The study of natural history stretches way back in history. As early as the first century AD, men like the Roman natural philosopher Pliny the Elder were examining plants in an attempt to understand their structure and life cycles. Early English naturalists include Thomas Penny (1530-1589) and William Turner (died 1568), respectively the first-known English lepidopterist and author of a book specifically on birds, but it was not until the late seventeenth century and the birth of the age of reason that the spirit of enquiry took hold and scientific natural history gradually gained in popularity. Not only did people observe the natural world around them more closely, but explorers increasingly started returning from their travels with plants and animals new to Europe.

The development of a system of classification by the Swedish botanist Carl von Linne (1707-1778), now more usually known as Linnaeus, was an important advance which enabled naturalists to bring order to their observations.

In England, the eighteenth century parson naturalist Gilbert White observed the seasonal patterns of plants and animals in his Hampshire village. Today, we read the *Natural History of Selborne* as a charming volume describing the times when White lived, but we owe him much more; he, as much as anyone, introduced us to the idea of observing nature. Making detailed observations and keeping records and drawing conclusions from them seems so familiar to us

Bluebell woodland at Powerstock Common.

43

Mary Anning, a pastel drawing by B. Donne.

now. It was a new concept, yet one which grew naturally out of Enlightenment thinking.

We can trace this rise in observational natural history in Dorset, and it is no surprise that it has been written about by a succession of distinguished naturalists. Over three centuries it is they who have laid the foundations of our knowledge of its rocks and fossils, plants and animals.

The continually eroding cliffs in the west of the county between Charmouth and Lyme Regis have long been known for their fossils and made famous by among others Mary Anning (1799-1847). She had been introduced to fossil collecting by her father. At that time there was a considerable market for fossils simply as artefacts which could be displayed. Their nature was not really understood. It was thought that they were pieces of rock which by chance had come to resemble plants and animals. It was to be a few more years before it was fully recognized that they were the remains of species which had formerly existed. It was William Smith, the geologist and originator of the first geological map of Britain, who pointed out that the various rock strata could be identified wherever they occurred by the characteristic types of fossils they contained. Not surprisingly, interest in fossils made Mary Anning famous. The coasts of Dorset have continued to be a paradise for geologists and palaeontologists, both amateur and professional, ever since.

Surprisingly however, there have been few other home-grown geologists who have achieved fame. Many of those who have studied and written about the county are from outside; the monograph on the geology of the western portion of the coast by Dr. W.J. Arkell is one such example. The distinguished geologist Dr. W.D. Lang, one time Keeper of Geology at the British Museum (Natural History) was another academic geologist who published regularly on the geology of the county. He did settle in the county and was President of the Dorset Natural History and Archaeological Society from 1938 to 1941.

Another contributor to the geology of Dorset was James Buckman (1814-1885). Born in Cheltenham, he held the chair of Geology and Botany at the Royal Agricultural College at Cirencester. In 1863 following a disagreement with a newly appointed principal, he resigned and settled at Bradford Abbas in north Dorset, 'where he took a large farm, which he conducted on model principles'. He studied the geology of the neighbourhood, which bore similarities to the oolitic limestones of the Cotswolds around Cirencester. He assembled a large collection of fossils and published regularly. He is also known for his agricultural research, especially for breeding new varieties of root vegetables. These plant breeding experiments attracted the attention of Charles Darwin as he was preparing *The Origin of Species* and Buckman and Darwin corresponded on these matters. Buckman was one of the founders of the Dorset Natural History and Archaeological Society, being its first Secretary and Editor of the *Proceedings*, which began publication in 1877.

The flora of Dorset has attracted botanists from as early as the sixteenth century yet

despite the richness of the flora the records were surprisingly few. We first find records of Dorset plants in the *Herbal* of William Turner in 1551-66. The first two editions (1774 and 1796-1815) of the monumental *History of Dorset* by the Revd John Hutchins contain plant lists by Dr. Richard Pulteney (1730-1801) of Blandford. It was not until 1870 that a full *Flora of Dorsetshire* was published by the Dorset-born botanist John Clavel Mansel (later Mansel-Pleydell) of Smedmore. Twenty years later a second edition was published. This was supplemented in the east of the county in 1900 by the *Flora of Bournemouth* (at that time in Hampshire) by the Revd E.L. Linton, Rector of Edmondsham.

It was to be almost another half century before a more modern account of the plants of Dorset became available. This was the work of Professor Ronald d'Oyley Good MA, ScD, FLS,

ABOVE The unstable cliffs at Black Ven, near Lyme Regis, where Mary Anning and her brother Joseph found the first complete ichthyosaur in 1811.
BELOW John Clavel Mansel-Pleydell.

ABOVE Professor Ronald d'Oyley Good.
ABOVE RIGHT The lizard orchid. It was his work on
the distribution of the lizard orchid that made Good's
reputation.

internationally renowned as a plant geographer. Good who is, perhaps, Dorset's most famous botanist, followed in the distinguished line of naturalists that the county has produced. He died at the age of 96 in 1992 having been born in Dorchester in 1896. Both his father and grandfather were doctors and practiced from the family home close to the County Museum in High West Street. Ronald Good was educated at Weymouth College and Downing College, Cambridge. During the First World War he was commissioned into the 4th Dorset Regiment and served in France. After graduation, in 1922, he took up a post at the British Museum (Natural History) and in 1928 moved to the Chair of Botany at the University of Hull. He remained there until retirement in 1959 when he returned to live in Parkstone. Good had known the County Museum since he was 10 years old. He was President of the Dorset Natural History and Archaeological Society (1961-64) and a Trustee of the Museum until his death.

Good was an outstanding botanical scientist and often ahead of his times in some of his thinking. In the 1930s he suggested that the affinities between the floras of Australia and South Africa could be explained by a theory of continental drift, yet it was not until at least the 1960s that continental drift became widely accepted as a theory. In a classic paper, Good linked the changes in the distribution of the lizard orchid (*Himantoglossum hircinum*) in southern England to climatic change during the early part of the twentieth century. In 1933 Good published *Plants and Human Economics* and in 1947 published *The Geography of Flowering Plants*. This work went through four editions and remains to this day a standard point of reference.

In 1948 the Dorset Natural History and Archaeological Society published Good's *A Geographical Handbook of the Dorset Flora*. This was and remains a unique work and was based on extensive research by Good in the 1930s in a project which he called the Botanical Survey of Dorset. Good's aim was to make a 'comparative study of the distribution within the county of as many as possible members of its flora . . .' To achieve this he aimed to record the species present at each of 8000 stands. The onset of war in 1939 curtailed his activities and so he only achieved 7575 stands. As Dorset is roughly 1000 square miles this is an average of 7 or 8 stands per square mile and with an average of forty species per stand the Survey contains a remarkable quarter of a million plant records collected entirely by Good between 1931 and 1939. From these data Good was able to assess which were the most abundant plant species in the county – namely Yorkshire fog (*Holcus lanatus*), followed by self heal (*Prunella vulgaris*), creeping buttercup (*Ranunculus repens*) and common stinging nettle (*Urtica dioica*).

Good then went on to show the distribution of the principal species in a series of 600 maps, all of which he plotted by hand. To locate each stand within the county Good had to devise his own grid system because he was working before the introduction of the Ordnance Survey National

A few of the Dorset flora recorded by the early naturalists.
Top left Toothwort, *top centre* Dyer's greenweed, *top right* Harebells, *centre right* Wooly thistle, a*bove* Nettle-leaved bellflower, and finally (*right*) one of Dorset's rarest flowers, the narrow-leaved lungwort.

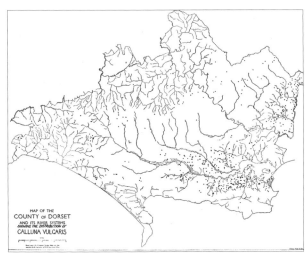

Ronald Good's maps showing the pattern of abundance of ling (above), which is confined to acid soils, compared with the hoary plantain (below), whose distribution is limited to calcareous soils.

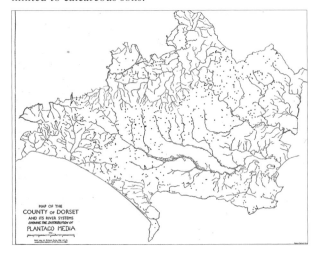

Grid, which was only finally established after the retriangulation 1936-1962. Good's grid reference system provides the same degree of accuracy as the now widely used six-figure national grid. He was then able to relate the distribution of the plant species to variations soil type and climate. The maps which Good produced, however, have frequently led to misunderstandings as to what he did and his results have been widely misinterpreted by modern botanists. The maps look similar to the now common atlases in which the occurrence of species is represented by a dot. However, because the stands are samples of the vegetation of Dorset, Good's maps do not indicate every occurrence of a species but show the pattern of their distribution and abundance. It seems that few field botanists today take the trouble to understand Good's methodology and have not read the detailed account, which he was careful to provide, in the *Handbook*. This seems to have been a problem in Good's own lifetime and to the end of his days he continually stressed what comparisons could and could not be made from his data.

Good's survey remains unique both in the breadth of its concept and the magnitude of the task. It would be daunting today to undertake this even with modern computing techniques. The Botanical Survey of Dorset was an exercise in what we would now call the processing of spatially referenced data; a procedure which with modern computing techniques has advanced considerably in recent years. Such procedures were unimaginable previously because we lacked the tools; however, Good both conceived this and carried it out. He was well ahead of his time. Now that we have the ability to make spatial studies our approach has changed and this is one of the factors which have led to what is now commonly called the 'living landscapes' approach to conservation.

Good's extensive travelling throughout the county gave him an unrivalled knowledge, from which he wrote *The Lost Roads of Dorset* in 1940, *Weyland: the story of Weymouth* in 1945 and in 1979 *The Lost Villages of Dorset*. Besides being a brilliant plant scientist he was at the forefront of the developing conservation movement in the 1950s and 1960s. He was one of the founders of the Dorset Naturalists' Trust and served as its first Chairman. The Trust also owes the acquisition of one of its finest reserves to him – Bracketts Coppice.

Good's *Handbook* remained the standard point of reference for the next 52 years although

James Charles Dale and Charles William Dale at Glanvilles Wootton.

The Lulworth skipper butterfly, named by James Charles Dale after a collecting expedition in 1832.

he did write a *Concise Flora of Dorset* in 1984; a revision of the plant list from his *Handbook*. During the 1990s under the leadership of Dr Humphrey Bowen (1929-2001), the plant recorder for Dorset, a team of field botanists covered the county accumulating new records of plants. The results of this survey appeared as the *Flora of Dorset* by Humphrey Bowen in 2000.

The climate and diversity of Dorset lies behind the richness of its insects and other invertebrates. These orders have attracted naturalists from the earliest of times, with butterflies predominating. The first of these entomologists was James Charles Dale (1791-1872) Squire of Glanvilles Wootton in the Blackmore Vale. He was one of the foremost field entomologists in England during the nineteenth century and added many new species of insect to the British list, most notably the Lulworth skipper in 1832. Dale was on a collecting expedition on Parley Heath in June 1820 with John Curtis, another leading entomologist, when he came across the orange-spotted emerald (*Oxygastra curtisii*) dragonfly, which he subsequently named after Curtis. The Moors River was long considered to be the haunt of the orange-spotted emerald but it has not been seen since the mid 1960s.

Dale began daily entries in an entomological journal at the age of 17 and continued to do so until the last day of his life in 1872. These diaries, together with his collections, are now in the Hope Museum at the University of Oxford. The diaries and other notes enabled his son Charles William Dale (1853-1907) to write the *Lepidoptera of Dorsetshire*. Besides his own and his father's notes this work contained records from the Revd O. Pickard Cambridge of Bloxworth, the Revd C.R. Digby of Studland and E.R. Banks of Corfe Castle.

The county was extensively studied by entomologists during this period and Digby and Banks published the 'Lepidoptera of the Isle of Purbeck' in the *Proceedings* of the Dorset Natural History and Antiquarian Field Club in 1885. Banks continued to collect notes with the intention of publishing a Lepidoptera of Dorset. However, ill health and his subsequent demise prevented this and the material passed to W. Parkinson Curtis (1878-1968) of Poole.

Curtis carried the work forward and finally published a 'List of the Lepidoptera of Dorset' in the *Transactions* of the Society for British Entomology in two parts in 1934 and 1937. Although Parkinson Curtis eventually

prepared a 650 page manuscript on the Lepidoptera of Dorset this was never published and remains in the Library of the County Museum in Dorchester.

It was not until 1984 when the Dorset Natural History and Archaeological Society published the *Butterflies of Dorset* by Jeremy Thomas and Nigel Webb that there was a book to match that of C.W. Dale published in 1886, almost a century earlier.

Less conspicuous groups of invertebrate received attention as well. The Reverend Octavius Pickard-Cambridge MA FRS (1828-1917), Rector and Squire of Bloxworth, was the world's foremost authority on spiders and related groups of invertebrates. Octavius Pickard-Cambridge was educated in Dorchester, where the Dorset dialect poet Revd William Barnes had been amongst his teachers. He first trained in law before going to Durham University to prepare for Holy Orders. After serving as a curate he returned to Bloxworth and succeeded his father as Rector in 1866. He had been interested in natural history from an early age. He first published a note on the willow warbler in 1852 and over the next 62 years he published almost 300 scientific papers and notes. Over half, 163, were on the Arachnida (spiders) but he published 52 papers on the Lepidoptera, 15 on other insect orders, 36 on mammals, 5 on reptiles, 4 were biographies, 2 were on the weather and 9 were on antiquarian topics.

He described many species new to Britain as well as many new to science. Among the former were two to which the name of the village of Bloxworth has become attached – the Bloxworth snout (*Hypena obsitalis*) a moth, and the Bloxworth blue (*Everes argiades*),

Lycæna argiades. *Pall.*
a,a. male; b,b. female.
Plant. Lotus major

F.O.P.Cambridge del.
E. Carter sc.

Mintern Bros. imp.

F. O. P. Cambridge del.
CORONELLA LÆVIS, ♀.
Mintern Bros. lith.

a butterfly now more usually known as the short-tailed blue. The Bloxworth snout, a rare immigrant, was found sitting on a post in the garden at the Rectory in 1884. This first record for the species in Britain was published in the Dorset *Proceedings* where it was accompanied by a full colour plate painted by Frederick Pickard-Cambridge, his nephew. A similar note accompanied the first capture in Britain of the Bloxworth blue. Pickard-Cambridge caught two individuals of this species on Bloxworth Heath in 1885.

Pickard-Cambridge also reported the first discovery in Britain of the smooth snake (*Coronella austriaca*) on Parley Heath. He was 'entomologising' with Frederick Bond when Bond captured the snake, which they both agreed 'was new to us'. An illustrated paper on this first capture and a description of the snake was also published in the *Proceedings*.

However, it is the spiders which accounted for most of Pickard-Cambridge's output of scientific

An engraving of the smooth snake published in the *Proceedings* of the Dorset Natural History and Antiquarian Field Club.

papers. He described and named many new species, not only from Dorset but from around the world. He published a book entitled the *Spiders of Dorset* in two parts in 1879 and in 1881. This book contained full descriptions of the species occurring in Dorset. However, the full title of the work was the *Spiders of Dorset with notes on species not found in the county*. It was, in effect, the spiders of Britain and held this position as a standard work of reference until superseded by a new monograph in the 1960s. His huge contribution to the classification of spiders was recognised in 1887 when he was elected a Fellow of the Royal Society. His contribution to taxonomy is still evident today. You will find 'OP-C' as the taxonomic authority cited after the scientific names of many species of spider and related invertebrates.

The raft spider found on heathland bog pools.

Pickard-Cambridge was a founder member of the Dorset Natural History and Antiquarian Field Club and was present at the inaugural meeting at the Digby Hotel in Sherborne in 1875. He was Treasurer of the Club from 1882 until 1899 and Vice President from 1883 until his death.

Pickard Cambridge was an early Darwinian and found in Darwin's *Origin of Species* views which very much accorded with his own. He corresponded with both Darwin and his fellow naturalist, Alfred Russel Wallace (1823-1913), the evolutionist and discoverer of the Wallace Line. Pickard-Cambridge's correspondence in the 1870s with Darwin concerned sexual selection and great differences in form between male and female spiders. There is also a connection between Wallace and Dorset. After expeditions to the Amazon and Far East, Wallace returned to England in 1862 and came to live in Dorset in 1889. He lived first in Poole, then built a house at Broadstone where he died in 1913. He is buried in Broadstone Cemetery.

Dorset can boast a long list of entomologists. We have already mentioned the Revd C.R. Digby of Studland, Eustace R. Banks of Corfe Castle and W. Parkinson Curtis of Poole. The Dorset-born Dr. C.D. Day (1885-1968), joined his father's practice in Dorchester and succeeded him as the Medical Officer of Health. An excellent entomologist he specialised in flies (Diptera) and is best known for his monograph *British Tachinid Flies*. Another medical man, although not born in Dorset, was Dr. A.A. Lisney (1907-1963). A keen all-round entomologist he concentrated on the Lepidoptera. He was a founder member of the Dorset Naturalists' Trust and succeeded Ronald Good as Chairman in 1962. For a number of years he was also Chairman of the Scientific and Conservation Committee of the Trust.

One of the most original entomologists the county has produced was Miss E.K. Pearce (1858-1940). Ethel Kathleen Pearce was born at Morden in 1858, the daughter of its vicar, the Revd Thomas Pearce. Pearce was a noted countryman and wrote frequently on field sports and country matters in *The Field* under the pseudonym 'Idstone'. His daughter was another of Dorset's keen dipterists and she contributed the section on flies in *A Natural History of Bournemouth and District* published in 1914 by the Bournemouth Natural Science Society.

She was also a pioneer in insect photography, and in 1915 Cambridge University Press published the first of three volumes of her pictures of British flies called *Typical Flies*. Each volume contained pictures of mounted specimens of about 150 species of fly. There were also pictures of the habitats and these are some of the few images of the countryside, particularly the heaths, from the early years of the twentieth century. In her preface to the first volume she remarks on the lack of 'elementary treatises' on the study of Diptera unlike the 'numerous manuals' dealing with Lepidoptera and Coleoptera'. Her book, she said, did not aim to fill that gap but she hoped that it would be 'of some use to the beginner . . .' These volumes were pioneering and it is from works such as these that the modern field guides, on which so many naturalists now rely, developed.

We have a distinguished roll call of Dorset naturalists. That many made contributions of national and even international significance is not surprising, given the great diversity of the county's wildlife. The earliest were often 'Gentlemen of Leisure' and of independent means. Nevertheless, they went about their studies in a thoroughly professional and academic way. Gradually, however, the balance shifted in favour of an increasing number of academic naturalists for whom natural history was a profession. These men and women, both locally and nationally, professional and amateur, were at the forefront of the new movement for the protection and conservation of wildlife which developed in the post war years. They were amongst the first to see that the changes in the countryside which began in the early decades of the twentieth century were inimical to wildlife and they were determined to do something about it.

THREE
A Conservation Movement is Born

With increasing numbers interested in natural history, geology and archaeology it was only a matter of time before they formed themselves into a society. The Dorset County Museum and Library had been established in Dorchester by 1845, but it was not until 1884 that its building, which it still occupies, was erected. On 16th March 1875 a group of about 20 naturalists met for dinner at the Digby Hotel in Sherborne and agreed to form the Dorset Natural History and Antiquarian Field Club. Its first President was the distinguished Dorset botanist J.C. Mansel-Pleydell and the Secretary and Editor of the *Proceedings* was Professor James Buckman. After a few years, the Field Club moved to Dorchester and established close links with the Museum. Eventually, the two

ABOVE The Marshwood Vale looking west from Eggardon Hill.
BELOW The Victorian Gallery, Dorset County Museum.

The Dorset heath, the largest British population of which is found in the county.

combined in 1928 as the Dorset Natural History and Archaeological Society.

In Dorset, as in most counties, the natural history society maintained a dominant position. Natural history was a scientific pursuit with its adherents not only recording what they found but attempting to understand their patterns of distribution and abundance. This stimulated a wider interest in the countryside and the protection of nature. The Royal Society for the Protection of Birds and the National Trust were founded in the late nineteenth century; the former in 1889 in response to the enormous killing of birds to supply plumes for ladies hats, and the latter in 1895 to protect notable landscape features.

Two factors were now at work. Growing numbers were reacting to the excesses of the industrialised society which had dominated the nineteenth century and sought to protect the places in which Britain's plants and animals were to be found. This philosophy was evident in other spheres, such as in the Arts and Craft Movement. It was at this time that the word ecology entered the language. It was coined by the German biologist and disciple of Darwin, Ernst Haeckel (1834-1919), and it has its root in the Greek word *Oikos*, meaning a house and is generally defined as the study of living organisms in relation to their surroundings.

The early years of the twentieth century saw not only the development of the new science of ecology but the advancement of the concept of nature reserves. The famous English botanist Professor Sir Arthur Tansley attempted to bring a focus to the new science and in 1904 called for the systematic survey and botanical mapping of the British Isles, and so was born the British Vegetation Committee. Once the surveying had been initiated it was necessary to implement its findings. For this a more formal body was needed, and one which was capable of dealing with the Government. The Committee became the British Ecological Society in 1913; the first learned society of its kind in the world.

Simultaneously, the Hon. Charles Rothschild (1877-1923), a leading entomologist, recognised that the best way to protect species was to safeguard the places where they lived. This concept led him to prepare a list of places that should be protected. He also envisaged that protection and the funds required would be achieved through a network of local wildlife trusts. To further his ideas he formed the Society for the Promotion of Nature Reserves (SPNR) in 1912 which received considerable support, including that of over 50 fellows of the Royal Society. He prepared a 'shopping list' of 284 'nature sites' which he submitted to the Board of Agriculture in 1915.

ABOVE Hambledon Hill from Hod Hill, one of 284 'nature sites' identified by the Hon. Charles Rothschild in 1915. The yew woods on its western flank is one of only a handful in Britain.

RIGHT Charles Rothschild formed The Society for the Promotion of Nature Reserves in 1912. It is now the Royal Society of Wildlife Trusts and the badger has been its emblem since 1970.

In Dorset, Rothschild's listed Ballard Down and its undercliffs, Bloxworth Heath, Hambledon Hill, Studland Little Sea, Lyme Regis Undercliff, Portland, and Wareham Heath. Rothschild's Society is still with us and about to celebrate its centenary. As wildlife trusts were formed they affiliated to the Society.

To stimulate the formation of wildlife trusts the SPNR formed a county Naturalists' Trusts' Committee in 1958 to provide a forum for the exchange of ideas, a means of representing common interests and as a body capable of negotiation at a national level. A.E. (Ted) Smith, a founder of the Lincolnshire Trust, was the Honorary Secretary of the Committee and he helped many trusts to come into being – including that in Dorset.

In 1970 the badger was adopted as the emblem of the SPNR and in 1976 the name was changed to the Society for the Promotion of Nature Conservation. There was a further change of name in 1981 to the Royal Society for Nature Conservation: it had originally received its Royal Charter in 1916. Since 2004 it has been the Royal Society of Wildlife Trusts and is the national body to which Dorset and 46 other wildlife trusts throughout the UK are affiliated.

To continue our history, we must, however, return to the early years of the 1920s. By now the conservation movement was gathering strength. An important turning point came when Scolt Head off the Norfolk Coast was acquired through an appeal to local naturalists who handed this reserve to the National Trust in 1923. However,

A bearded tit, characteristic of the reed beds round Poole Harbour.

In 1941 the SPNR promoted conferences on 'Nature Preservation in Post-war Reconstruction'. The Government then added to its Standing Committee on National Parks a further committee – the Nature Reserves Investigation Committee. The members of this Committee were for the most part leading ecologists. The Chairman was Dr. Julian Huxley, but he was succeeded by Professor Sir Arthur Tansley. A key member of the Committee was a senior civil servant with Dorset connections, Captain Cyril Diver.

Cyril Diver (1892-1969) grew up in Parkstone and after reading zoology at Oxford he became a Clerk to the House of Commons. The generous recesses of the House provided Diver with time to pursue ecological research. In the 1930s he initiated and led one of England's foremost ecological surveys on the Studland Peninsula at the mouth of Poole Harbour – the South Haven Peninsula Survey. From his boyhood home in Parkstone, he had frequently walked this area and knew exactly what it held. The South Haven Peninsula Survey became a classic piece of ecological research which continued throughout the 1930s until curtailed by the outbreak of war. Diver, as one obituary pointed out, achieved more as an amateur than many achieve as a professional.

The deliberations of these wartime Committees resulted in a far reaching White Paper published in 1949. The vision that it embodied was remarkable. Its authors sought not only to protect places which they regarded as essential for the pursuit of ecology, but also to establish a countryside full of wildlife for the benefit of everybody. They regarded it as almost a right, and that society would be all the better for it – a far-sighted even idealistic aim to have had during the dark war years.

The 1949 White Paper led to the setting up of a network of National Parks, National Nature Reserves and Sites of Special Scientific Interest,

when the National Trust was unable to accept Cley Marshes in 1926 a 'Naturalists' Trust was set up to own and maintain the reserve. Soon the view was expressed by the distinguished plant ecologist F.W. Oliver that he would look forward to the time when every county would have its own Trust; very much echoing Rothschild's original aim. Meanwhile, the SPNR had acquired Woodwalton Fen in Cambridgeshire in 1919; its first reserve and a gift from Rothschild.

So we see the initial growth of a movement for the establishment of nature reserves and for bodies to own and manage them. However, much more needed to be done, but by the end of the 1930s Britain was once again at war. During the years that followed two initiatives went ahead. There were organizations such as the Ramblers Association whose principal concern was outdoor amenities and recreation in the post war years. Lined up with them was the Council for the Preservation of Rural England (CPRE) and the SPNR who sought the same for the protection of nature.

as well as the formation of a state agency to establish nature reserves, conduct ecological research and promote nature conservation. So the Nature Conservancy (now called Natural England) came into being. As both an ecologist and a first class administrator, it was no surprise that Diver was appointed its first Director General.

The Committee laid down the principle that nature conservation was to be practiced with a sound basis in ecological science. However, it also recognized that ecology was still a young discipline and that investment in research was needed. So, besides its conservation activities, the Nature Conservancy was charged with leading ecological research.

A search began for suitable locations for the Conservancy's first two research stations. Here Diver's experience and influence came into play. From his Dorset boyhood and research at Studland he knew that the Isle of Purbeck was one of the most biologically rich places in the whole of Britain. Thus one of the two was located at Furzebrook. The Research Station soon became well-known both in Britain and internationally as a centre of excellence in conservation research, a position it retained until government reorganisation resulted in its closure in 2000 – just short of its fiftieth anniversary.

The Norfolk Naturalists' Trust had been formed in 1926, but it was not until 1946 that the next, in Yorkshire was formed, followed by Lincolnshire in 1948. In 1956 further Trusts were formed in Leicestershire, Cambridgeshire and the Isle of Ely, followed in 1957 by the West Midlands (Warwickshire, Worcestershire and

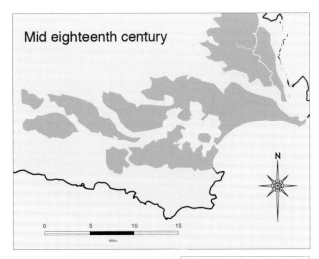

Mid eighteenth century

One of the key reasons behind the birth of the Trust was the gradual loss of heathland in the south-east of the county. The map above shows the extent of the mid eighteenth century heath, the one on the right the remaining pockets in 1978.

Staffordshire), by Kent in 1958 and Surrey in 1959.

The Trust movement gathered momentum and by the end of 1962 almost every county in England had a Trust or was in the process of forming one. The impetus of the 1949 Act and the evident changes in the countryside had energized this movement. The growing threats and dangers were clear as was the need to take action not only nationally but locally. Dorset was already at the forefront of nature conservation in Britain and Cyril Diver was among those who were founder members of the Dorset Naturalists' Trust. This leads us on to the next chapter in our story – the founding of Dorset's own Trust.

FOUR

The Call to Arms

The post war years saw the landscape of Britain change, as urban development and its associated infrastructure expanded. Agriculture and the ways in which the land and stock were managed similarly changed. The public demanded a reliable and plentiful supply of home-produced food at acceptable prices. The new farming practices involved taking more land into cultivation and the increasing use of synthetic fertilisers, chemical pesticides and herbicides.

Dorset was less affected by some of these changes than other parts of the country, nevertheless, the decades of the 1950s and 1960s saw considerable losses of heathland and downland. The heaths of east Dorset which in the mid eighteenth century extended of some 40,000 hectares had been reduced to about 10,000 hectares by 1960. These losses were in part due to the expansion, from the

LEFT A view over Powerstock Common looking west towards Pilsdon Pen and Lewesdon Hill.
BELOW Harvesting in about 1900 at Bere Regis.

Contrast this photograph of a recently harvested field near Bere Regis with the one on the previous page. The trend towards larger fields with few hedgerows and weeds has been to the detriment of wildlife. The vivid yellow of oilseed rape has become increasingly common recently.

Rare and endangered species of the Heath.
Top left Black bog ant.
Top centre Bog asphodel.
Top right Cotton grass.
Left Pale heath violet.
Lower left Bog pimpernel.
Right Heath lobelia with large skipper butterfly.

mid nineteenth century onwards, of Poole and Bournemouth, as well as extensive planting of conifers and the ploughing of heathland. Today, the extent of the heathland is barely 15% of that in the eighteenth century.

The losses of chalk downland have been even more drastic. The permanent grassland on the downs was converted to arable farming and the growing of cereals. Only in the Great Vales was the impact of what was in effect an agricultural revolution less noticeable. Here dairy farming persisted. Likewise, in remote parts of of west Dorset traditional farming practices persisted, keeping the small scale landscape largely intact.

In the post war years these changes led to concern that 'natural habits of scientifically interesting plants and animals were fast disappearing', and that the existing organisations were not well equipped to counter this change. Various discussions took place, particularly between Miss Helen Brotherton and Brigadier Charles Hall Woodhouse, who was at that time President of the Dorset Natural History and Archaeological Society. So it was in late 1960 that an announcement was made by a new organisation calling itself the Dorset Naturalists' Trust. The announcement is illustrated on the opposite page, and note that the final paragraph, with almost Churchillian tones, was underlined to emphasise its importance.

This new Trust had an interim Committee of which the Earl of Ilchester was President. Sir David Williams Bart and A.D. Pass OBE, DL, JP were Vice-Presidents. Professor Ronald Good MA ScD FLS was the Chairman and Brigadier C.H. Woodhouse OBE MC DL JP and A.J. Bull MA were Vice Chairmen. The Honorary Secretary was Miss Helen Brotherton of Canford Cliffs.

So it was, on Tuesday 28th March 1961, that the Inaugural Meeting of the Dorset Naturalists' Trust was held in County Hall, Dorchester. Admission was free and the speakers were E.M.

Nicholson CB, the well-known ornithologist, who had succeeded Cyril Diver as Director General of the Nature Conservancy; A.E. (Ted) Smith, Honorary Secretary of the Naturalist' Trusts' Committee of the Society for the Promotion of Nature Reserves, and Dr Norman Moore, then the Regional Officer for the South West of England for the Nature Conservancy based at Furzebrook Research Station.

The Trust was incorporated on the 31st March 1961 the Subscribers being listed as *Charles Hall Woodhouse, Retired; Ronald d'Oyley Good, Emeritus Professor; Kenneth Basil Rooke, Medical Practitioner; Norman Ingram Hendy, Civil Servant; Ernest Walter Baldwin Gale, Superintendent of Parks; Arthur Ernest Howell, Bank Manager; Arthur Jarvis Bull, School Master; and Helen Alice Jane Brotherton, Spinster.*

OPPOSITE PAGE The 'Call to Arms'.
BELOW Inaugural Meeting on 28th March 1961.

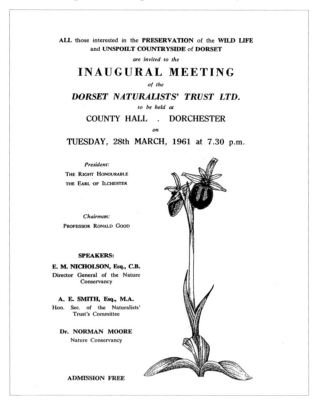

ALL those interested in the PRESERVATION of the WILD LIFE and UNSPOILT COUNTRYSIDE of DORSET
are invited to the

INAUGURAL MEETING
of the
DORSET NATURALISTS' TRUST LTD.
to be held at
COUNTY HALL . DORCHESTER
on
TUESDAY, 28th MARCH, 1961 at 7.30 p.m.

President:
THE RIGHT HONOURABLE
THE EARL OF ILCHESTER

Chairman:
PROFESSOR RONALD GOOD

SPEAKERS:

E. M. NICHOLSON, Esq., C.B.
Director General of the Nature Conservancy

A. E. SMITH, Esq., M.A.
Hon. Sec. of the Naturalists' Trust's Committee

Dr. NORMAN MOORE
Nature Conservancy

ADMISSION FREE

THE DORSET NATURALISTS' TRUST

Under the sponsorship of the Dorset Natural History and Archaeological Society, an independent Committee has been formed for the purpose of setting up a Dorset Naturalists' Trust. The Committee wishes to acquaint you with what is being done and to enlist your support.

The main objects of the Trust are to prevent the unnecessary destruction of the County's wild plant and animal life, and to help preserve places of special natural history interest, for the benefit of future generations.

Although Dorset has to some extent escaped the worst effects of urbanization and similar development, certain types of natural habitats of scientifically interesting species of plants and animals are fast disappearing. Neither the Nature Conservancy nor any other existing organisation is able to cope with this problem on the County scale.

Further serious encroachment on Dorset common lands and wild places should be resisted. Those who genuinely desire to preserve the natural features of the County must take positive action to safeguard them. To this end, it is proposed to incorporate the Trust as a limited company and to circulate as widely as possible an informative brochure setting out the aims and objects and appealing for support.

A Public Meeting will be convened in the Spring of 1961 to inaugurate the Trust when it is hoped that the maximum number of interested people will be enrolled. The initial stages will involve a certain amount of expense which it is hoped will be defrayed by enrolling Founder Members (annual subscription £1) and Founder Life Members (compounded subscription £15). In the case of pre-payment by Founder Members, membership will date from the Inaugural Meeting.

The following bodies are among those who have promised support:- The Nature Conservancy, The Dorset Branch of the Council for the Preservation of Rural England, The Poole and District Natural History Society, The Purbeck Society, The Dorset Field Ornithology Group, The Portland Bird Observatory, The South Dorset Bird Watching Society, The Dorset Wildfowlers' Club, and the Wimborne Historical Society.

This first appeal for practical support is being made mainly to naturalists so that through them a much wider public may be reached.

The need is urgent and the task extensive, and positive action is necessary if the objects of the Trust are to be achieved. As a first step, you are invited to write to the Secretary and enrol as a Founder Member.

Publications to celebrate the fifth, tenth and twenty-fifth anniversaries of the founding of the Trust.

The first Newsletter of the Trust, a single foolscap side, was issued in July 1961, together with a membership list. Membership had increased steadily and there were 306 Founder Members of which 71 were Life Members. The interim committee became the first Council of the Trust, although there were some small changes. Professor Good had been replaced as Chairman by Arthur Bull, and became a Vice Chairman. The Honorary Treasurer was P.A. Bently. The Ordinary Members of the Council were L. Abbott, R.E. Beddingfield, W.S. Best, O.N. Blatchford, A.F. Chapman, R.F. Dalton, E.W.B. Gale, Sir Rupert Hay, N.I. Hendy, E.G. Hyde, Dr. A.A. Lisney, R.N.R. Peers, J.E. Roberts, Dr K.B. Rooke, and Miss E.M. Samuel. Dr Lisney was to Chair a Committee to make recommendations to the Council on matters relating to conservation. This early Council met first at Wollaston House in Dorchester, now the Headquarters of the National Farmers' Union, but soon moved to the School Room of the County Museum where it continued to meet for over 30 years until the Trust acquired its permanent headquarters at Brooklands Farm.

Members were informed that the Trust was already negotiating to safeguard several important areas, but it would not be expedient to mention these in this Newsletter. However, members should look forward to exciting news in the next Newsletter. It concluded with a call to enroll further members and with the fine exhortation 'We in Dorset must protect Dorset'.

Although there were a number of individuals involved in founding the Trust, the driving force was Helen Brotherton. She had two great passions, an avid interest in natural history, particularly in birds and flowers, and sailing: Dorset was one of the few places where both could be satisfied. Helen had moved to Canford Cliffs with her parents after the Second World War on her father's retirement from business in the Midlands. Helen was a prominent figure among the naturalists in the county and clearly understood that what was needed to ensure the future of its wildlife was a conservation Trust.

As a teacher before the war, she had encountered the pioneers of the Trust movement in Norfolk and particularly, A.E. (Ted) Smith in Lincolnshire. He was a great influence on her, instilling the need to set up a body able to own and manage nature reserves. To do this, her formidable organising skills were brought into play. These she had honed during the war as the WVS Evacuation Officer for Warwickshire.

Like a number of other such women her war work had enabled her to recognise the potential of her talents and to trust her own judgement. She had an innate ability to see the way forward and was seldom wrong; she had the managerial skills to make things happen. At first she had considered entering politics, but in this she was deterred by the more extreme she encountered. Politics loss was nature conservation's gain. Helen was a formidable organiser. In no time, she brought together a group of like-minded people to form the Dorset Naturalists' Trust.

Not content with that, she was simultaneously involved in saving Brownsea Island in Poole Harbour. This resulted in the National Trust acquiring the Island and the subsequent arrangements that gave the Wildlife Trust one of its first and finest reserves.

Not surprisingly Helen served on many Committees, including the Councils of the National Trust, the Royal Society for Nature Conservation and the Royal Society for the Protection of Birds. Her involvement in local activities included many years' service on the Poole Magistrates Bench, while all the time acting at the Hon Secretary of the Dorset Naturalists' Trust; a job which was, in effect, that of its Director.

Over the years, the Trust's volunteers were its driving force. Helen had a unique ability to

Helen Brotherton, the driving force behind the Trust from the beginning.

identify the right person for the job in hand, and to persuade them that they were indeed exactly the right person to do it: furthermore they always had her support.

Helen was one of the pioneers of wildlife conservation in Britain. Her work was recognised by the award of the CBE in 1984. She was the third person to receive the Christopher Cadbury Medal from the Royal Society for Nature Conservation in 1992, and in 2007 she received the Octavia Hill Medal from the National Trust. However, it is here in Dorset that are her tangible and lasting achievements; saving Brownsea Island, the founding of the Dorset Wildlife Trust and the establishment of the Portland Bird Observatory.

FIVE

Protecting our Wildlife

The objectives of the Dorset Naturalists' Trust were *'to preserve the wild plant and animal life of the county; to protect the wild places, heathlands, unspoilt coastline and other areas of scientific importance, which are the natural habitats of plants and animals, so that the heritage we now enjoy shall remain for future generations; to promote and encourage the study of natural sciences with particular reference to the opportunities offered by Dorset.'*

The new Trust's first Newsletter in July 1961 announced that negotiations were in hand for several important sites and that there would be more in the next Newsletter. The second Newsletter in February 1962 announced that a reserve had been established at Ridge near Wareham to protect the location of viper's grass (*Scorzonera humilis*). The site at Ridge was one of only two locations in Britain at which this member of the Compositae family of plants grew.

Botanists have always been uncertain as to whether viper's grass is native here and it may have been introduced. Ronald Good in his *Geographical Handbook of the Dorset Flora*

LEFT Brownsea Island from the air, showing the lagoon and the marsh and reed beds in the centre of the Island.
RIGHT Viper's grass at Arne, protected by the first reserve created in February 1962.

Marsh gentian.

suggests this. In conversation with the author in the late 1980s Ronald Good said he thought it may have been introduced as a contaminant of seed when Ridge was cultivated during the First World War. He was unaware of the presence of the plant before the war but it was present afterwards.

Despite its origins the plant needed protection and the reserve had been set up by agreement with a local farmer. The Newsletter described this as a common practice used by county trusts. Indeed, it was, and many of the Trust's early reserves were established by such means. It was to be a few years before the Trust owned a reserve and even longer before it made its first purchase.

The second Newsletter also indicated the Trust's other plans. The first was for a reserve on an area of heathland in the east of the county. By the next Newsletter in July 1962 the Trust had a reserve on 50 hectares of Cranborne Common leased from Lord Cranborne. This was an area of heathland which had been left unplanted with conifers. It was a site where Montagu's

harrier and Dartford warblers bred and where marsh gentian could be seen. It was a fine piece of heathland that remained a Trust reserve until 2003 when the lease expired. In the early years Cranborne Common was threatened by a massive overhead power line, but objections by the Trust resulted in its diversion.

However, by far the most important issue was the future of Brownsea Island in Poole Harbour. The Island had come on to the market at almost the same time as the formation of the Trust as a result of the death of its reclusive owner, Mrs Mary Bonham Christie. Helen Brotherton was a keen yachtswoman, annually sailing her X-class boat at Cowes Week for many years. Sailing enabled her to clandestinely explore Brownsea and she soon realised the importance of the island and the need to maintain it as it was for nature conservation. She then encouraged various parties, especially the National Trust, to save the Island and was behind the efforts to raise the necessary funds. An endowment of at least £100,000 was needed to maintain the Island; Helen raised £10,000 in the first week alone.

In late 1961 several members of the Naturalists' Trust's Council visited Brownsea Island at the

Helen Brotherton sailing her X-class boat at Cowes in 1962.

Dartford warbler.

invitation of Mary Bonham-Christie's grandson. The second Newsletter, on February 1962, reported that there was no matter of greater concern to the newly formed Trust than the fate of Brownsea. The discussions were helpful but negotiations about the future of the Island were complicated. Throughout the proceedings the Trust had championed the case for the retention of the Island in its present state. The Trust also made known to the various parties involved its willingness to co-operate in the management of the undeveloped parts of the Island, provided a settlement could be made which prevented further development.

The National Trust became the owner of the Island. As 'it was largely on the initiative of the Naturalists' Trust that Brownsea Island was saved for the nation', discussions then followed for the Naturalists' Trust to have two reserves. The larger, on the north side of the Island, was to include woodland, the marsh and the lagoon, and was of great ornithological interest. There would also be a smaller reserve on the southern shore to preserve gravelly exposures of importance to insects. Both of these reserves would be looked after by members.

The outcome of the discussions resulted in the Dorset Naturalists' Trust leasing 125 hectares of saltmarsh, freshwater marsh, two freshwater lakes, sea shore, heath and mixed woodland on the northern part of the Island. However, the proposed second reserve on the south of the Island did not materialise. The area leased included the large Victorian house known as the Villa. The reserve was primarily a bird sanctuary with great numbers of wildfowl and waders in winter and a safe breeding place, including an heronry, for many species in summer. Red squirrels were also present on the Island.

The remainder of the Island would be managed by the National Trust. The DNT would pay a peppercorn rent to the NT and to maintain a

Brownsea Island's wildlife includes (*left*) avocets, (*centre*) Sandwich terns and (*bottom*) red squirrel.

nature reserve to which the public would have access under supervision. These early Newsletters were written by Helen Brotherton herself and went on to state very clearly the role the Trust had on Brownsea. 'The Dorset Naturalists Trust has played a very prominent part in securing Brownsea for the nation and it will be preserved for ever as a place where the public may enjoy peace and tranquillity and where birds and animals which find sanctuary there can be studied by naturalists. The responsibility that this will entail for the Trust and its members must not be shirked.'

Arrangements were made for members to visit Brownsea on 13 Oct 1962. On this occasion 150 members, almost half the total membership, attended. They were able to view the Villa, which was in the centre of the reserve, and to see the work required to accommodate a warden and to provide other facilities. It was intended to have the reserve open to visitors by the spring of 1963 and to fill the post of warden. Volunteers were required to clear scrub. The area had become invaded with dense thickets of rhododendron, whose clearance was to continue for the next fifty years, led by the indomitable Betty Savage. Arthur Walton was appointed as Honorary Warden-Naturalist and together with his wife moved into the Villa.

Lady Baden-Powell opened the Island on 18 May 1963. She recalled that she knew the Island well as she was married in Parkstone and lived for her early married years at Evening Hill overlooking the Harbour and the Island. Also, it was on Brownsea that her husband had held the first Boy Scout camp in 1907, which in turn led to the birth of the Scouting Movement.

The Waltons stayed until October 1964 when they were replaced by Mr Lionel Patten and

Kevin Cook installing the first wind pump to control the lagoon water level.

1966 the advertisement in the Newsletter, so typical of those times, sought 'a young man keen on some branch of natural history who is waiting to go to university'. During the winter of 1968 management plans were developed in conjunction with the Nature Conservancy and the Royal Society for the Protection of Birds not only for the Trust's reserve on Brownsea, but also for the various reserves around the Harbour.

At this time, Mr and Mrs Patten left Brownsea and the Trust appointed Tony Wise as Reserves Warden. His title implied that he was not only responsible for Brownsea but had overall responsibility for the scientific work on all the Trust's reserves. The Trust had received a grant from Carnegie Trust for 3 years (£500, £400, £300). So the Trust had its first full time employee. Nevertheless, a retired couple were still needed to live at the Villa and maintain the pump and generator and Landrover and act as caretakers. This fell to Mr and Mrs C. Leng who remained until 1975. Mains electricity was needed in the Villa and an appeal was made to Trust members. Tony Wise left in 1984 and was succeeded by Kevin Cook who had been an assistant summer warden at various times since 1976. Kevin remained until 2000, when once again a former assistant, Chris Thain, was his replacement.

When Kevin started in 1984 he found that there was much to do in addition to the management of the reserve. The Villa was in a poor condition, and a water treatment plant needed installing. During Kevin's time many of the improvements that we now enjoy were put in motion by him. The lagoon which provides such a valuable habitat for the large numbers of waders that visit the island is dependent upon a water pump and sluice gate which simulates a tidal effect. Initially power was provided by a wind pump which Kevin made himself. Then in 1995 this was replaced by a submersible electric pump, the funds being provided in memory

wife. By now Brownsea was attracting attention beyond the Trust and successful open days were held and a Landrover donated. In the meantime volunteers continued the hard work of clearing scrub and repairing buildings. One of the problems on the Island was the dense population of mosquitos. The principal species involved was the saltmarsh mosquito, *Aedes detritus*, which bred in the marshes of the Harbour and was a problem in some of the surrounding areas as well as on the Island. In December 1963 the Trust received a grant from the Nature Conservancy to employ an entomologist to study the problem. M.W. Service took up this position in March 1964 and was based at Furzebrook Research Station of the Nature Conservancy.

Although there was an honorary warden in residence on the reserve the Trust also employed a summer warden to assist with visitors. In

Volunteers tackling the major task of clearing rhododendron which infested the whole Island.

The island suffered in the severe gales of 1987 and in particular 1991, when many of the Scots Pines were destroyed and the 'Mac' hide had to be retrieved from the middle of the lagoon. In recognition of the subsequent restoration work done on the woodlands for the benefit of the Red squirrel population, the Forest Authority 'Forest of Excellence' award was given to the Trust. This work included creating deer exclusion areas to control damage by the large Sika deer population.

The 'Mac' hide owes its existence to a founder member and one of the earliest and keenest volunteers on Brownsea, C.R. Macdonald, or 'Mac' as he was known. He became aware of the Trust through an advertisement in the local press for people to support the funding of the Trust and at once enlisted. He was involved in a number of businesses, including selling tropical fish. He enjoyed hard work and spent his summers as a volunteer assistant warden on Brownsea, where he pioneered the building of tern islands in the lagoon. However, the Trust did not have the resources to employ him full time and he subsequently became the National Trust Warden on the Golden Cap Estate. Here he continued to support the work of the Wildlife Trust by arranging leases on parts of the estate for reserves and by undertaking almost all of the printing and stationery requirements of the Trust, selling Trust goods and helping in countless ways.

of Ray Ellis by his father. Ray was one of the many volunteers who Kevin encouraged and who helped him with the many tasks. Bill Oddie on one of his several visits described this as a 'wonderful feat of ornithological engineering.' Another volunteer who sadly died young was Colin Reid, whose father set up a trust fund in memory of Colin which helped to provide for a number of key projects.

A major task was to clear the enormous amount of rhododendron which infested the island. This work was helped by many volunteer work parties, including employees of some of our key corporate supporters – such as Barclays on their 'community make a difference day'.

Mac died in 1985 and in his memory, the construction of a hide facing the northern half of the lagoon began. The construction was inaugurated by David Attenborough when he visited in November 1985. The hide was sited to enable visitors to have good views of the Sandwich tern colony and the waders and wildfowl visiting the lagoon in both summer and winter. After some eighteen months of 'dogged' construction the hide and its causeway was completed and officially opened in April 1987 by Sir Joseph

Destruction of the Scots pines by the severe gale in 1991.

TOP The 'Mac' hide extends well into the lagoon.
ABOVE LEFT C.R. Macdonald, known as 'Mac', centre, with Helen Brotherton, right, in the early 1980s.
LEFT Helen Brotherton with Sir Joseph Weld who opened the original 'Mac' hide.
ABOVE The hide had to be replaced and was opened by Simon King in November 2010.

Weld. The tern islands have been a great success. When the reserve began there were no more than half a dozen pairs of nesting terns; today there are 450 pairs of two, sometimes, three species. After many years of service the hide needed refurbishment; this was completed with a grant from the Heritage Lottery Fund during 2010. The new hide was opened in November 2010 by the broadcaster and naturalist Simon King.

The first little egrets to be reared in the United Kingdom were on Brownsea Island in 1996.

Spring snowflake a great Dorset rarity.

Little egrets were seen on Brownsea as long ago as 1970 when there were 7 or 8 individuals in Poole Harbour; the first sightings for over a century. By 1989 they began to be seen in increasing numbers and in 1996 the first pair to breed in Britain raised young on Brownsea Island. Since then, the number of breeding birds has increased considerably. They are to be seen widely in Poole Harbour and in the river valleys of Dorset and their range in Britain has continued to expand.

At the same time that the Trust was involved with Brownsea it established two more reserves, at Cranborne Common in the east, and Brackett's Coppice near Corscombe in the west. It is to Ronald Good that we owe Brackett's Coppice. In 1961 he and Helen Brotherton were travelling down to west Dorset to visit the site of the spring snowflake (*Leucojum vernum*). In passing, Good suggested a short detour to see a fine ancient woodland and coppice with a rich flora, which was the site of a variety of the wild crab apple (*Malussylvertris* var. *mitis*). It is impossible to imagine their dismay when on arriving at the wood they found a large area had been felled in preparation for planting with conifers and that the Forestry Commission had plans to clear fell all of Brackett's Coppice.

Helen Brotherton recalled in later years that so incensed was Ronald Good, an otherwise mild mannered man, that he 'danced with rage' in the road; a saying Helen had heard but never before witnessed. She went to work straight away and negotiated with the Forestry Commission and Corscombe Estate a lease on the remaining portion of the coppice, which in 1963 became a reserve with potential for educational work. The lease was renegotiated for a further fourteen years in December 1966. Eventually when the Forestry Commission was compelled by the then Government to dispose of some of its holdings, the Trust was able to purchase the reserve in 1985 with funds from the Trust's Silver Jubilee Appeal.

Today, Brackett's Coppice is one of the finest of the Trust's reserves. It is an area of sloping woodland with a rich ground flora and noted in the autumn for its fungi. The woodlands slope down to a fast-flowing stream. Adjacent are hay meadows which are cut annually, and these together with coppiced areas are rich in butterflies. This is a particularly good area for species of fritillary, but sadly the pearl-bordered fritillary is no longer present despite research into its habitat requirements which were too late to save it.

More recently, in 2002, the Trust was able to acquire Birch Common, adjacent to Brackett's

Coppice, which had been felled in the early 1960s and planted with conifers. The Trust set about removing them and has now successfully restored the species rich grassland typical of this part of west Dorset.

From the earliest days the Trust was interested in Powerstock Common, but it was not until 1964 that it was able to secure a management agreement with the Forestry Commission over 20 hectares of rough grassland, typical of west Dorset, which the Commission had left unplanted. Eight years on, following further negotiations, the Trust leased just over 50 hectares from the Forestry Commission of ancient oak woodland and scrub. The then Chairman of the Scientific Committee remarked in the Annual Report that 'Now is the time for members in West Dorset to show that they can be as enthusiastic woodlanders as the active

TOP LEFT Mrs Shepherd and her daughter picking primroses on Birch Common in 1962, before it was planted with conifers.
TOP RIGHT AND ABOVE The conifers being felled by the Trust in 2004, and the area before restoration to grassland began.
BELOW A similar area cleared of pines in 1988 on Powerstock Common has been restored back to a fine species rich pasture.

band who look after Brackett's Coppice'.

In 1980 the Trust was able to purchase a portion of the disused railway line which bordered the reserve on its northern side, the grassy banks of which were rich in butterflies and orchids. Eventually, with funds from the Silver Jubilee Appeal the Trust was able to purchase the remainder of the 985 year lease on a substantial area of Powerstock, including the ancient woodland and coppice, the grassy areas and some of the plantations. It was also able to purchase 12 hectares of the adjacent Stones Common. Over the years since the plantations, mostly of Sitka spruce, have been removed and the ancient grassland restored. Besides these fine reserves in the west of the county the sale of land by the Forestry Commission at this time enabled the Trust to acquire reserves at Hurn on the Moors River.

The early Trust reserves were acquired through conservation management agreements. The Trust itself did not own a reserve until 1965

The disused railway line crossing Powerstock Common was purchased by the Trust in 1980, and is a valuable habitat for orchids and butterflies.

when Mrs Aswin made a gift of 16 hectares of woodland – Holway Woods – to the Trust. This remains a Trust reserve and is a fine area near the village of Sandford Orcas and on the border with Somerset. In the spring the flora, dominated by bluebells, is spectacular.

The first reserve to be purchased by the Trust was of 3.5 hectares at Stonebarrow Hill adjacent to Newlands Batch near Charmouth. It was bought in March 1969 with the help of a grant from the Pilgrim Trust of 10% of the cost. The 50 or so hectares which formed the Newlands Batch Reserve were managed under agreement with the National Trust's Golden Cap Estate.

In these early years the Trust managed several reserves owned by the National Trust, these included Black Ven, beneath which Mary Anning made her famous discovery of a fossilised *Ichthyosaur*, and The Spittles. While further eastward around Golden Cap, the Trust established reserves at Newlands Batch and St Gabriel's Bank. Near Ringstead there were agreements over land at Whitenothe and Burning Cliff. There was also an agreement with the landowner for a reserve of marshy ground behind Chesil Beach at West Bexington. In these years the Trust had considerable holdings on the coast. Elsewhere in the county, reserves included areas of heathland in the east, calcareous grasslands and quarries in Purbeck; the habitat for rare species of bat.

At the time of its tenth birthday in 1961 the Trust was managing 24 reserves covering almost 400 hectares; however, only two of these were owned – Holway Woods and Stonebarrow Hill.

By the time of its Silver Jubilee, in 1986, the number of reserves had risen to 40, covering over 1000 hectares.

The long dry summer of 1976 is remembered for the heathland fires which swept through a number of nature reserves in the east of the county. At this time, the Trust bought 35 hectares of chalk downland at Fontmell Magna from the Springhead Estate. A further 46 hectares were bought by the National Trust. The Dorset Naturalists' Trust was able to lease from the National Trust a further 35 hectares of the south

ABOVE Byron Henry is one of many dedicated volunteers who has been leading work parties on the reserve at Holway Woods for many years.
BELOW Holway Woods gifted to the Trust in 1965.

Two of the many fungi that are found in the woods of West Dorset, Elf cups and bracket fungus.

facing slopes above Longcombe Bottom. The purchase was assisted by a grant for £1500 from the World Wildlife Fund, and a year later a grant from the Nature Conservancy Council paid for the fencing on the reserve. At this time the reserve was known as the Springhead Reserve, but today we know it as Fontmell Down.

In 1986 the Trust was alerted by its Reserves Officer, Richard Jennings, to the fact that Lower Kingcombe Farm near Toller Porcorum in west Dorset was coming on to the market. 'Here in spring and summer the fields and hedgerows fill with colour from an abundance of wild flowers. The meadows teem with butterflies and other insects while all around there is a rich and diverse bird life. The fields are small and bounded by hedgerows with ancient oaks and form a mosaic of pasture, woodland and bog. Much of west Dorset would have been like this in the past as Arthur Wallbridge, who, until his death at 94, had continued to farm in the only way he knew. He did not enlarge the fields, re-seed pastures or spray harmful chemicals and fertilisers. Hidden in the folds of the hills, this is an idyllic place, frozen in time and rich in wildlife.'

Negotiations to secure the land by the National Trust and other parties had been going on for two fruitless years. The main stumbling block was the provision of sufficient funds to secure the future management of the area. Then suddenly on the day the Trust Council was meeting to discuss its position it was announced that the land would be put up for auction in six weeks' time. There was

Kingcombe Meadows Nature Reserve acquired by auction in 1987.

no time to be lost; there was an instant decision to launch an appeal. In her usual way this was led by Helen Brotherton. The Appeal got off to a good start when the artist Gordon Beningfield, who was particularly fond of this part of Dorset, donated a painting to be raffled. However, the Appeal was haunted by the thought that it would be possible to collect money but fail to buy at auction. So, donors were asked for pledges to be redeemed if the bidding was successful. The money then began to come in. One member of the Trust staff was happily surprised when asking a stranger on the telephone what amount they had in mind to donate was told £50,000. Grants were lined up in no time at all from the Countryside Commission,

Dorset County Council, the Landmark Trust, the National Memorial Heritage Fund, the Nature Conservancy Council, the West Dorset District Council and the World Wildlife Fund. John Paul Getty contributed £89,250 through the British Wildlife Appeal and the Duchy of Cornwall promised to provide fencing and gates for the future reserve. In all some £300,000 had been raised or pledged. Meanwhile, the flower-rich meadows had been notified as a Site of Special Scientific Interest by the Nature Conservancy Council.

The day of the auction arrived. The Corn Exchange in Dorchester was packed to capacity not only with farmers, bidders and other spectators, but also television crews and reporters. The Trust's Honorary Land Agent, Bill Humphreys, rose notably to the occasion and the bidding began. At the end of the day the Trust had secured six of the fifteen lots on offer amounting to 164 hectares. Other Trust members, including Nigel Spring and Peter and Judy Westgate through the Leggatt Trust had secured further lots, including Home Farm, Beech Cottage, Sunnyside Cottage and Fisherman's Cottage. Just over a month later a celebratory picnic was held at Kingcombe which was attended by over 700 members.

The auction over the work began. Richard Jennings, the Reserves Officer and champion of Lower Kingcombe, set to work to plan its management by continuing the traditional method of farming that had produced such an abundance of wildlife. There were further appeals, so that Pound Cottage could be restored for a Warden, for the purchase of a tractor and trailer and other equipment. Further small areas have been added to the holding and this is now one of the finest reserves anywhere.

The farm buildings and adjacent land, which had been purchased by other individuals, were converted and opened as a residential field studies centre in 1988 by Nigel Spring, and the Kingcombe Trust was established to operate this enterprise. In 2010 the Kingcombe Trust merged with the Dorset Wildlife Trust, enabling the promotion of conservation, sustainable development, and other forms of environmental education activities at the Centre to be expanded.

Heathland is one of Dorset's principal habitats. A few years after the acquisition of the reserve at Cranborne Common the Trust added to its holding by taking up a management agreement with the Forestry Commission for Woolsbarrow in the heart of Wareham Forest. The Trust is no longer responsible for either, but it is not without heathland reserves. In 1980 the Trust acquired through a lease a fine area of heathland and riverside meadows and marsh at Tadnoll. In the 1990s the Trust purchased the adjoining Winfrith Heath, when the Atomic Energy Authority divested itself of surplus land. Other heathlands have also been acquired at Sopley, Upton Heath, Coombe Heath and Higher Hyde. In all the Trust has some 480 hectares of heathland reserves.

The first of the Conservation Studies, published by the Trust in 1974 on Marine Wildlife Conservation in Dorset, contained the ambitious recommendation, originated by its author John Hawthorn, to set up a marine nature reserve. In 1980 the Kimmeridge Marine Reserve, the first of its kind on a mainland shore in Britain, came into being. It extended from Clavell's Hard on the east side of the bay to Warbarrow Tout. Mrs Sarah Welton was employed during the summer as the marine reserve warden. All this was possible through the financial assistance of Major J.C. Mansel, who was the owner, the Countryside Commission, British Gas Corporation, British Petroleum and the World Wildlife Fund. In addition to the reserve the Trust opened an Interpretative Centre in a large fisherman's hut. This housed displays on the history of Kimmeridge Bay and the marine life to be found there. Over the years this proved to be an extremely successful centre.

In 2003 the facilities at Kimmeridge were improved and a splendid new centre – the Fine Foundation Marine Centre – was opened. The generous funding from the Fine Foundation has enabled the marine conservation activities to continue at Kimmeridge. Today, the Trust has four staff dedicated to marine conservation and the operation of the Centre at Kimmeridge.

Besides the large reserves the Trust also has a network of smaller reserves throughout the county, including two old orchards, Broad Oak Community Orchard near Sturminster Newton given to the Trust in 1979, and King's Lane Community Orchard at Powerstock. Both contain old varieties of apples. The old wood in the trees provides valuable habitats for many insects and other invertebrates, whilst the surrounding grasslands are rich in plant species. Other small reserves include Mill Ham Island in the River Stour given to the Trust in memory of Mrs Myrtle Cousins, 'a much loved member', by her daughter Mrs C. Scott and Mrs Angela Hughes, who had each owned part of it. Sutton Holms of only 0.8 hectares is a traditional pasture with a small pond, marsh and woodland. Collyer's Brook (0.81 hectares) near Fontmell Magna is a series of ponds supplied by spring water.

At the present time the Trust manages 42 reserves covering an area of 1300 hectares. Over the years the holdings of reserves have changed. In the early years most were either leased or held under management agreements with their owners as the Trust did not have sufficient funds to make outright purchases. Many of the early reserves, particularly on the coast, were held under management agreements with the National Trust. Over the years, with the exception of Brownsea, these agreements have been relinquished and the land returned to the National Trust. This was a satisfactory arrangement as the National Trust developed its own capability to manage the land for wildlife conservation. By so doing the Trust has released resources to be used elsewhere on its reserves. In a number of other cases, where leases have expired, the land has returned to its owners. This is similarly a satisfactory arrangement as such areas are now often notified Sites of Special Scientific Interest and have an acceptable degree of protection and access to funds for management. Today, almost all of the reserves are owned by the Trust and a full list with details of what can be found is included at the end of this book.

At the time of the founding of the Trust nature reserves were seen as the principal method of conservation. This concept has a long history stretching back to the late nineteenth century. Many early nature reserves were chosen because they represented fine examples of particular plant and animal communities; others were the locations of particular rare species. What they had in common was their scientific importance and this was because they were, for the most part, selected by ecologists and naturalists.

A consequence of this approach was the insistence that the public should be excluded, that nature should be allowed to flourish, and that we humans should only look in from the outside. We were not part of the system, merely its managers. This approach was very much to the fore in the Trust's early reserves. The reserves leaflet produced at the time of the Tenth Anniversary of the Trust indicated that access to almost all reserves was by permit only. In only a few cases where public footpaths crossed reserves were members able to visit. Collecting and observing the species present was almost entirely banned. This resulted in a stifling of the pursuit of scientific natural history, a practice which has largely been reversed in recent years. Although the conservation movement recognized the need for a scientific basis for its decisions it was, nevertheless, often wary of study and research being carried out on its own reserves.

Today things are different. Public access to almost all reserves is encouraged and welcomed. There are a few restrictions such as limits to horse riding or control of dogs to protect breeding birds or stock. Reserves are no longer seen as the principal means of promoting conservation. The last 25 years have seen an increasing recognition of the concept of the living landscape. This approach has developed out of our understanding of habitat fragmentation.

We once tended to see nature reserves as little more than a picture of nature with a static character. We now regard landscape as a working entity in which people are one of the components. The concept of cultural landscape of the past has now been reshaped into that of a 'living landscape'. We have developed a more satisfying approach in which man and wildlife exist side by side in an integrated system. This recognises the dynamics that characterise the interactions between species populations and landscape elements; a feature lacking in the protected area approach to conservation.

The concept of a 'living landscape' is now widely accepted as a way forward for conservation. The idea of providing links within the landscape between protected areas has long been advocated, but had not really taken hold in practical conservation work until recently. We have a poor knowledge of how species disperse within a landscape, for it is a subject which is difficult to study. Even if we provide links we cannot tell whether species will use them, even if, intuitively, we feel this should be the case. The substantial network of reserves held by the Trust provide the nuclei from which species can spread out into the surrounding areas. The Trust now tends to acquire reserves only when they complement the existing network and contribute to its 'living landscapes' policy.

The rare marsh fritillary butterfly.

SIX

A 'Living Landscape'

Throughout the life of the Trust there has been a strong emphasis on volunteering. Helen Brotherton led by example, devoting literally thousands of hours to the work of the Trust without any financial reward, and she expected a similar level of commitment from others. In Helen's case the Trust almost dominated her life. For its first 16 years it was run from Helen's house, Island View, in Canford Cliffs.

In these early years the Trust was managed by its Council with an Executive Committee. From the beginning, there was a Scientific Committee whose main responsibility was to identify species and communities throughout the county in need of conservation. They were the main forum for choosing reserves and specifying their management. Each reserve had a local management committee who carried out conservation management tasks and field recording. By 1969 the Council felt the need to set up a publications committee, and to consider the appointment of a paid warden for Brownsea and an assistant secretary. As we have already seen, A.J. Wise was appointed as the Reserves Warden and was based on Brownsea.

However, the Trust was growing and the Council decided that a full time Conservation Officer was required. Up to now these duties had been shared out among the volunteers who served on the Conservation Committee. The County Council approved a grant to the Trust

Purbeck Marine Nature Reserve at Kimmeridge was the first voluntary marine reserve in the country.

87

to meet the first three years cost of employing the Conservation Officer. Unfortunately, there was a delay, so Mrs Dorothy Holmes stepped in 'like a fairy godmother' and gave £1000 so that the appointment was not held up. Mrs Holmes was also responsible for providing the Brownsea Island Endowment Fund.

In September 1973 David Venner was appointed as Conservation Officer. Sadly, his tenure was short and he was succeeded by Ian Soane in October 1974. The Soanes settled in Bere Regis. Once again Mrs Holmes came to the rescue and helped them buy a house to be used as a conservation office.

In June 1976 a full time Administrative Officer was appointed. Col F.D.M. Warne at first worked from Island View, but as the Trust was growing rapidly the Council felt that a permanent headquarters was needed. Members were asked through the Newsletter to help locate a suitable property, preferably within reasonable reach of the main centres of population. It was suggested that this might be perhaps a small holding or farm, which could be converted into offices and a Countryside Centre, perhaps by a river or with an area suitable to make a lake. Helen Brotherton remarked that we need have looked no further than the Villa on Brownsea Island had it been on the mainland. Various avenues were explored, often at the suggestion of members, but in the end the Trust settled for renting three rooms in the building owned by the Bournemouth Natural Science Society at 39 Christchurch Road in Bournemouth, into which the Trust office moved in May 1977.

Bournemouth was not altogether the best location within the county and, to counter this, a contact point for members was established in Dorchester. The Conservation Officer continued to work from home organizing the work on the reserves through the local management committees. The main office was supported by a team of volunteers. In the early years,

the volunteers who served on the Council and various committees were, in effect, the Trust staff. It is important to recognise that so much was achieved by this network of volunteers.

Don Warne retired at the end of the 1977 and was succeeded by Mrs Margot Pike.

The following years saw further additions to the staff. There was a warden, Sarah Welton, for the marine reserve at Kimmeridge and there was a part time publicity officer. Dr Lesley Haskins acted as honorary Scientific Consultant, thus relieving the Conservation Officer of the ever growing burden of dealing with planning matters. Throughout the early 1980s the Trust was able to take advantage of various Government schemes for job creation. Temporary staff were taken on principally to manage the reserves, but also to make surveys, especially of the marine areas, and to work on publicity material. At times, up to 40 temporary members of staff were employed through these schemes. Much of the day to day staff management rested with the Conservation Officer, but later it was possible to employ a team manager through the scheme.

From the earliest years of the Trust each reserve had a management committee of locally-based members. These members knew the reserves intimately and, under the guidance of the Scientific Committee, developed plans and managed the reserves. They were helped on occasions by the Dorset Conservation Corps; a team of mostly young people who were available throughout the county to undertake conservation management work, such as scrub and tree removal.

The Trust continued to acquire reserves. These were both larger and of higher quality than many of the early reserves. During this period some of the early reserves which were held under agreements from the National Trust were returned; this was especially the case in west Dorset. At the same time, the existing reserves were being improved by the management teams.

As this created a greater work load for the Conservation Officer, it was decided to create a separate post of Reserves Manager. In 1985 the Trust was able to secure funding from British Petroleum, who were then developing the Wytch Farm Oilfield, and appointed Richard Jennings as Reserves Manager. This made possible considerable growth in the management of the reserves, especially at Powerstock and Brackett's Coppice. The Trust was about to acquire the substantial reserve at Kingcombe Meadows, involving traditional methods of farming and it was not long before a warden, Paul Comer, was appointed.

With larger and more prestigious reserves to manage the role of local management committees declined. Much of the management of the reserves now fell to full time wardens employed by the Trust. Eventually, in early 2000 the network of reserves committees was wound up.

Kingcombe Meadows Nature Reserve was the first reserve where traditional methods of farming were introduced for the benefit of wildlife.

This was a period when the Trust underwent a major overhaul of its governance and the whole committee structure of the Trust was modified, bringing it into line with the best practices for the management of a charity.

The growth in the Trust in the 1980s required further office accommodation, mainly to meet the needs of the conservation staff. In 1983 two rooms were rented in Dorchester in Trinity Street. Then in early 1985 the office moved to slightly more spacious accommodation in High East Street 'down the passage between the knitting wool shop and the washeteria!' The Conservation Officer was based here, as was a new Projects Officer, Jane Franklin. Soon this accommodation was insufficient and the Trust

The Trust logo is based on the very rare early spider orchid, which only occurs on some sites in Purbeck.

purchased a charming Georgian terraced house in North Square into which the Dorchester-based staff moved in February 1988; the central administration, however, remained in Bournemouth.

Having been founded as the Dorset Naturalists' Trust in 1961 by the time of its Silver Jubilee in 1986 it was felt that a new name was required. There had been discussions as early as 1965 that the name should be the Dorset Trust for Nature Conservation. The original name reflected the ethos of the times in which the Trust was founded, but attitudes and aspirations had changed. It was much less about meeting the needs of scientific natural history and more about conservation in the countryside as a whole. There was considerable debate as to whether it should be the Dorset Trust for Nature Conservation or the Dorset Wildlife Trust. The latter term was just beginning to be taken up by some of the county trusts. However, it was one step at a time, and the vote went in favour of the Dorset Trust for Nature Conservation. Whilst this still remains the formal name of the Company, since 1994 the Trust has operated under the name Dorset Wildlife Trust, bringing it into line with the 46 other county Trusts.

From its very beginning the Trust adopted the early spider orchid (*Ophrys sphegodes*) as its emblem. What plant could be more evocative of the county than this orchid? A beautiful and detailed drawing of the entire orchid plant appeared on the original announcement of the formation of the Trust and on the first four Newsletters and other publications. This design was the work of Julie Gooch. The lip of the flower bears a strong resemblance to the body of a large fat brown garden spider. It is one of Britain's rarest orchids and is confined to calcareous soils in the coastal counties of Kent, Sussex and Dorset; the population in Dorset being amongst the largest. It is one of the earliest of British orchids to flower and can be seen from mid-April until the end of May on some of the Trust's reserves.

By mid-1963 the emblem had changed; only the flower of the orchid was used and this was encircled by the words Dorset Naturalists' Trust and early spider orchid. This design was also converted into an enamel badge for members. This version lasted until the early 1980s when it was replaced by a reworking of the orchid flower and the removal of the encircling lettering. The emblem underwent further revision by Christina Hart-Davis in the 1990s before a new design was adopted in 2008. This incorporated the orchid flower in a stylized form into a design which evoked the landscape of the county.

For the first 25 years of the Trust Helen Brotherton, although titled Honorary Secretary, was in effect its Director. In 1986 she became its Chairman. Eventually, in 1990 she became President and a new Chairman, Alan Swindall, was elected who continued very much in the role of Director.

Despite the strong attachment to the volunteer ethos, it was increasingly evident that the work and growth of the Trust was being held back by the lack of a suitable headquarters and a full time Director. Eventually, in 1995, almost 35 years after its formation, the Trust appointed its first Director; Dorset being one of the last of the county trusts to do so.

The first task for the new Director, Nick Coombe, was to resume the search for an headquarters. All the early attempts were unsuccessful and matters were beginning to look desperate. At last, a suitable property,

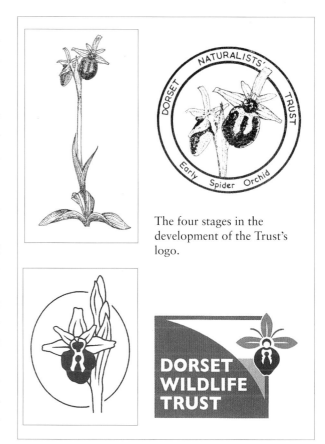

The four stages in the development of the Trust's logo.

Brooklands Farm, at Forston, just to the north of Dorchester was bought in 1995. To provide funds the Trust launched a successful appeal to members, which was masterminded by Mrs Jo

The Dorset Wildlife Trust's Headquarters and Conservation Centre at Brooklands Farm near Dorchester.

A large pond was created at Brooklands, lined with old carpets supplied by members, the photograph below shows the pond as it is today.

pond that was created is filled from rainwater collected from the roof of the centre and stored in an underground tank buried beneath the car park. This again has been highly successful and boasts a good population of southern marsh orchids on the pond edge.

Not only was this to be a headquarters but it was planned as a conservation centre. The idea was not new, but it was not until the formation of Public Relations Committee in 1969 that it developed. This Committee was formed to make the Trust's work and objectives better known. Despite the many activities which by now had developed for members, which included meetings, film shows, open days and other events comparatively very few people at that time had any idea about the Trust's activities.

The Committee's original plan was for a Countryside Centre, however, this evolved into a mobile centre in what became known as 'The Caravan'. This travelling exhibition and sales outlet transformed the image of the Trust, keeping it in the public eye and interpreting the Dorset countryside for 'the interested visitor'. It took for its slogan that from the American National Park Service – 'through interpretation understanding; through understanding apprec-iation; through appreciation protection'.

The caravan was acquired for £3500 with a grant for 75% of the cost from the Countryside Commission. It first appeared at the Blue Pool in

Davis. Beside the farm there was land for car parking and an arable field which it was planned to restore to chalk grassland.

This 1.5 hectare field was deep ploughed and then sown with seed collected from the nearby National Nature Reserve at Hog Cliff Down. This restoration has been highly successful and is a fine example of how chalk downland flora can be brought back again. There is now a fine display of cowslips and many other chalk downland plants, including orchids. The adjacent

The caravan, once a familiar sight throughout Dorset.

Modern displays and shows are regularly put on by the Trust.

Lorton Meadows Conservation Centre.

August 1972. It soon had a full itinerary and every year would visit suitable locations, particularly the agricultural shows. For many years it spent the winter in the grounds of Furzebrook Research Station, and teams of volunteers were organized to staff it during the summer. The original caravan was eventually replaced by a larger one but sadly this was destroyed in a road accident. It was not replaced as by now the Trust headquarters provided a conservation centre, together with the centres which have gradually opened over the years on Brownsea, Kimmeridge, Beacon Hill, Lorton, Kingcombe, with a further one planned for Chesil. Modern travelling displays and tents are now available for shows and other locations.

With a permanent headquarters and full time Director the Trust began a period of substantial growth. This period coincided with many funding opportunities from government schemes particularly agri-environment programmes. Other opportunities included the Landfill Tax and funding from the National Lottery. Other funds became available from Government agencies such as English Nature, the Environment Agency and local authorities, as well as from other charitable Trusts.

Lorton Meadows to the north-west of Weymouth had long been a conservation issue due to the intention to construct new roads into Weymouth. The Trust acquired the meadows and a derelict barn, and with funds from the Heritage Lottery Fund set about creating a conservation centre to serve the needs of Weymouth, Littlemoor and Preston. In 2004 the then Member of Parliament for South Dorset, Jim Knight, opened the new centre, which now provides a full programme of recreational and educational activities throughout the year.

In 2002 the long established marine centre at Kimmeridge was enlarged and refurbished, with a new building with excellent display areas, acquaria and a live underwater camera. The refurbishment was aided by a generous grant from the Fine Foundation and the new centre opened in 2003 as the Fine Foundation Marine Centre. It maintains a full programme of courses and information for both the general public and school and college groups.

On Brownsea the Villa has undergone refurbishment with much improved sleeping quarters and better displays. On the reserve there has been much work and after fifty years of toil the invasive rhododendron has almost been eliminated. On the lagoon the hide, originally erected in memory of the energetic volunteer

The Kingcombe Environmental Studies Centre.

C.R. 'Mac' Macdonald, has been rebuilt.

In the east of the county the Trust has been able to establish a base at Beacon Hill at Upton in a building made available through the generosity of the Beacon Hill Brick Company. This provides a base for the Trust wardens for the nearby reserve on Upton Heath and for a team developing conservation in the urban area and working with groups of disadvantaged people.

The Kingcombe Environmental Studies Centre merged with the Trust in the autumn of 2010. The merger has placed the Wildlife Trust with its extensive and fine reserve at Kingcombe in a position to develop further its activities in west Dorset. In 2012, hopefully in time for the Olympics, the Trust plans to open the Chesil Centre near Portland Harbour. This is a joint enterprise with the Ilchester Estate, the Fine Foundation, the Weymouth and Portland Council and the Heritage Lottery Fund.

The Trust began in March 1961 with 306 Founder Members. By February 1962 the second Newsletter reported that membership had grown steadily and was now over 400. The first Annual General Meeting was held at the Corn Exchange Dorchester in July 1962. It was attended by about 150 members and a further 200 had sent good wishes. By 1965 membership had exceeded 700 and at the Sixth Annual General Meeting in July 1967 the 1000th member had been enrolled. The President presented Miss E.M. Barber with an inscribed copy of Keble-Martin's illustrated *Flora of the British Isles*. Membership reached

1600 by the time of the AGM in 1970. On reaching its tenth year the Trust hoped to have 2000 members. This landmark was achieved in October that year when Mrs D. Thresher became the 2000th member and was also presented with a copy of Keble-Martin's *Flora*. Writing in the Newsletter, Helen Brotherton remarked 'It took us six years to reach the first thousand; four years to reach the second; dare we hope it will be only another two before we attain 3000?' This prediction was almost fulfilled and the 3000 mark was achieved in 1974 and 4000 by 1981.

By the time of the Silver Jubilee AGM in 1986 membership had reached 5000 and Mrs Frieda Sutton was presented with a book on Nature Reserves. For the next fifteen years membership continued to grow; the 8000 mark was achieved in 2000 and the 10,000th member enrolled in 2002.

From this point the Council took the decision to actively recruit members. Although the Trust had grown as a business it was largely as a result of income from external sources for specific projects. Subscription income, which maintains the core activities of the Trust, had not increased at the same rate and there was an imbalance. Active recruitment enabled the Trust to increase its membership to 20,000 over the next five years. The 25,000th member was enrolled in 2007. Membership continued to rise, reaching almost 27,000 but has now fallen slightly and hovers at just over 25,000.

In 1961 the annual subscription was £1 and this did not rise to £2 until May 1972. It rose further to £3 in 1978. The rise from £2 to £3 was justified by the then Treasurer in the September 1977 Newsletter in the following terms. 'If the subscription was worth £2 when it was last increased in 1973 it must now be worth only 60p. Looked at from another point of view what is £2 worth? A bottle of wine or six pints of beer or 60 cigarettes or 7oz of Nescafe or 2lbs of bacon or a shampoo and set. All are things which can be drunk, smoked, consumed or washed away in a short time. The Trust gives lasting value and the crux of the matter is how many members are prepared to go out and enlist new members'.

Today the minimum subscription for a single membership is £32.

At the Annual General Meeting in July 1964 it was resolved to introduce a Junior Membership for those under 18 years or up to 23 if in full time education at a subscription of ten shillings (50p) per year. This move resulted in the formation of Dorset Young Naturalists (DYNats). The aim was to enable them to take an active part in the work of the Trust. It was hoped that these junior members would join working parties on reserves, sponsored litter collections, walks to

A recruitment newsletter from 1985.

A junior Watch Group visits Lorton Meadows and inspects a laid hedge.

raise funds and indoor meetings. This junior membership continued for a number of years. However, it biggest problem was finding adult members to plan and organize the activities. The Newsletters contained frequent appeals for volunteers to help. In 1976 it joined Watch, the national group for the young begun by the umbrella body for the county trusts, the Royal Society for Nature Conservation. For many years the Dorset Watch group was active and run by a long standing volunteer, Mrs Pat Mills.

Besides holding and managing reserves, the Trust has, from the very start, sought to influence policy and decision making in relation to conservation, not just locally within Dorset but nationally. In its first Newsletter the Trust reported that it had successfully challenged an application for planning permission to build a petrol filling station on land adjacent to the newly opened Portland Bird Observatory. From the very start, this established the Trust's role as an organisation able effectively to lobby on behalf of Dorset's wildlife. Since then, the Trust has acquired a highly professional reputation in the field of planning and development control. Two years later a similar application at Portland was successfully opposed. At the same time the Trust expressed its concern about cars driving on

to Chesil Beach between Abbotsbury and Burton Bradstock and damaging the flora.

Nationally too, the Trust was concerned that the legislation relating to Sites of Special Scientific Interest needed strengthening. The Trust made representations to the SPNR to raise this with the Government. Locally, this was an issue as considerable areas of chalk downland were being lost through changing farming practices.

However, two issues were to dominate these early years – toxic chemicals and human population growth. The publication of Rachel Carson's *Silent Spring* in 1962 was hugely influential at a time when many counties were forming their Trusts. Already in the first Newsletter, members were urged to pressurize the Ministry of Agriculture into restricting the use of chemical pesticides on spring sown crops. The second Newsletter highlighted the dangers to wildlife, particularly to birds where there had been widespread deaths caused by the use of chemical pesticides. The Trust had joined in making representations to the Ministry of Agriculture to restrict their use. Members were asked to look out for corpses which might have been poisoned and to send them to the RSPB, who would forward them to the Nature Conservancy Toxic Chemicals Unit at Monks Wood for chemical analysis to determine the cause of death. This topic continued to occupy the Trust during its first ten years.

Concern for national, if not international issues, was evident at the tenth Annual General Meeting in July 1971 when a group of members raised a motion concerning the effects of human over-population. No punches were pulled. Control of human populations, it was maintained, was the single most important issue facing conservationists. The Trust should urge the Government to investigate all means of stabilizing and reducing the population of England. That this issue was raised was very much in keeping with the thinking of the early

1970s. Environmentalists feared that global population growth was a major danger and that the sheer weight of numbers would exhaust the planet's resources in as little as thirty years. Interestingly, it is an issue which once again is much in the news.

Another early success story by the Trust was the publication of a series of reports entitled *Studies in Conservation*. The first of these was 'Marine Conservation in Dorset', written by John Hawthorn and published in 1974. Again this was a ground-breaking enterprise and was published to national acclaim. It provided the blue print for the pioneering achievements of the Trust in marine conservation. The study summarized the results of at least two years survey work on the marine resources of the county. It proposed the setting up reserves both to protect the marine flora and fauna and to educate the public. It also stimulated the other Trusts in the south-west to work together in achieving marine conservation.

In the discussions which followed reserves were proposed for Kimmeridge Bay, and the Fleet and Chesil Beach. There then followed a

ABOVE The rock pools at Kimmeridge Bay are rich in marine wildlife.
BELOW A brittle star.

further series of underwater surveys of marine life which provided a sound scientific basis for marine conservation. For these surveys the Trust was able to take advantage of funding through various initiatives from the Government for job creation. By 1978 the Trust was in a position to establish the marine nature reserve in Kimmeridge Bay, described in the previous chapter.

ABOVE A beautiful rock pool at Kimmeridge exposed at low tide.
BELOW The Fleet and Chesil Beach with Portland Bill in the distance.

The Fleet, which lies behind Chesil Beach, was another area which the Marine Study identified as of importance. The Ilchester Estate, which has owned Chesil Beach and the Fleet, including the famous Swannery, for five centuries, established the Fleet Sanctuary Trust in 1975. It recognized that increasing disturbance and pollution threated this unique wetland. The Naturalists' Trust was represented on its management committee. The Fleet Trust enabled a warden, Don Moxom, to be employed mainly to protect the colony of little terns which nested on the beach. These arrangements have remained in place until the present time.

In addition, the Fleet Study Group was formed, which although not a Trust initiative has involved a number of its members. Its aims were primarily scientific and intended to gather knowledge about the Fleet. The Group has met regularly over the years, producing scientific reports on many aspects of the ecology and physiography of the Fleet and Chesil Beach.

The second of the Conservation Studies that the Trust published was 'Wildlife Conservation in the Poole District and Poole Harbour'. This report was in two parts. The first by W.G. (Bunny) Teagle was concerned with the urban area and highlighted the natural history importance of areas such as Upton Heath, Creekmoor Ponds, Canford Heath, Bourne Bottom and Talbot Heath. The second part of the report dealt with Poole Harbour itself and was compiled by W.O. Copland. While proposing conservation policies on the whole Harbour it focused particularly on protecting the southern part of Poole Harbour. These policies were widely adopted and remain influential today; they were particularly important when the Wytch Farm Oil Field was developed in the 1980s. These two highly successful studies were followed by ones which focused on the Avon Valley, Bournemouth and Christchurch.

The 1970s were dominated by a number of planning issues and the Trust was increasingly involved in submitting evidence to various Structure Plans within the county. The Chairman of the Scientific Committee, E.D. Le Cren, explained in the 1973 Newsletter that the Trust took a public stand where necessary. For example, at Portland there was a dispute over the removal of 150 tons of pebbles a year. While this was a small amount compared with elsewhere on Chesil Beach, the Trust felt it needed to draw a line and resist the removal of material from the beach unless scientific evidence demonstrated irrefutably that there was no risk to its structure.

A further example was Poole Harbour. Here the planning authority had been sent a memorandum that emphasised the need to secure a balance between the parts of the Harbour used intensively for commerce and leisure and the parts that should be carefully protected for wildlife, peaceful enjoyment and visual amenity. This of course reflected very much the recommendations that the Trust had made in its own report on Poole Harbour. A proposal to

extract gravel and sand at North Bestwall and Swineham near Wareham ignored the need for a proper long term plan in which conservation was given priority. The Trust believed that this, together with the Swineham-Keysworth-East Holton areas, should receive stringent protection. Similarly, the Purbeck shores of the Harbour required to be protected.

The Trust was also involved with other conservation bodies in the Working Party to advise on the proposed opencast ball clay mine on the Arne Peninsula. The Dorset County Council rejected the planning application and this immediately led to a Public Inquiry being held in December 1975. The Conservation Officer, Ian Soane, who was new in the post found himself busy preparing the Trust case that there should be no commercial development on the peninsula. The Trust's case was prepared in collaboration with other conservation bodies, particularly the RSPB. Soon after the Inquiry opened it emerged that the Nature Conservancy as a result of conditions in other leases in the area was obliged to withdraw their objection. The burden of defending the peninsula then fell to the non-statutory conservation organisations. In the event the Inquiry was lost and clay mining went ahead, nevertheless, this proved to be a valuable experience for the Trust in defending important wildlife sites at an Inquiry.

These skills were soon to be needed as from the middle of the decade we began to see the development of the Wytch Farm Oil Field. A small oil well had operated at Kimmeridge since the 1950s. This was as much an attraction as it was a commercial enterprise, as it was sited on the top of the cliffs overlooking the bay. However, the 1970s saw exploration for further oil deposits a mile deep in the rocks beneath the southern shores of Poole Harbour and under Poole Bay. This saw the development of a number of wells along the southern shore of the Harbour and a rail terminal for transporting

the oil at Furzebrook. The pipeline across the heathland was one of the first examples where detailed restoration procedures were developed to ensure the re-instatement of the heathland vegetation.

It was when further oil wells were proposed, including one on the Goathorn Peninsula, that the County Council proposed the setting up of a panel – The Goathorn Inquiry – to take a more strategic view of the oilfield development and its affects on the environment of Poole Harbour and its hinterland. The Wildlife Trust was the only non-statutory body invited to sit on the team; the others being the County Council, Purbeck District Council, Wessex Water and the Nature Conservancy Council.

The Inquiry reported in 1979 and laid the foundations for further development of the oilfield. Throughout the early stages the field was developed by British Gas, but after the Government compelled what was then still a nationalised industry to sell its oil exploration arm, it was developed and operated by a consortium of companies led by British Petroleum. From then on environmental issues were thoroughly examined and solutions developed in consultation with conservation bodies, especially the Wildlife Trust, and with professional ecologists. The development of the oilfield was achieved with great sensitivity to the wildlife of the area. It also resulted in research into methods of ecological restoration for a number of plant and animal communities which have now become widespread standard practices.

From its beginnings the Trust has always sought good relations with the farming community within the county. Many prominent landowners and farmers were among the founders of the Trust. One of these, Mrs Angela Hughes, who farmed at Hammoon in the Blackmore Vale, was a leading figure at the first national conference on Farming and Wildlife held at Silsoe in

Bedfordshire in 1969. This was a ground-breaking conference, coming as it did after the excesses of intensification and the use of toxic chemicals that characterised the 1960s.

From out of the Conference came the Farming and Wildlife Advisory Service (FWAG), which is still with us and which works closely with the Trust in Dorset. Angela Hughes saw that what was needed was a follow up conference to be centred on a working farm and which would demonstrate that it was possible to farm, as she did, in a way beneficial to its wildlife. The following year she organised the second national conference in Dorset. This was attended by 160 delegates and was based at Weymouth College with sites visits to her own farm. Ten years later in 1980, she organised a follow-up conference attended by some 225 delegates to assess the progress at Hammoon.

These conferences set the scene for excellent relations between the Trust and the farming community ever since. In February 1976 a Liaison Committee between the Trust and the National Farmers' Union was set up. Farming was changing and many of the new methods being introduced were seen as inimical to wildlife. The Trust established the post of a Farming Liaison Officer, strengthening the links with the farming community and advising on grants under various agri-environement schemes. Today, the Trust meets farmers through its Agriculture Panel where major issues are debated.

Over the years, a recurring problem has been the issue of badgers and bovine tuberculosis. This came to prominence in the 1970s and has in the spotlight ever since. Western Purbeck was a trial area for a campaign to remove badgers to see if outbreaks of tuberculosis could be controlled, but the Dorset badger population has continued to increase and outbreaks of tuberculosis still occur in cattle. Both pose a considerable policy problem for the Wildlife Trust movement nationally.

A dormouse. Regular checks on dormice populations are carried out by Sue Eden and other volunteers.

SEVEN

Into the Future

After 50 years, what is the Dorset Wildlife Trust like today compared with 1961? Many features remain the same, but in many other spheres the organisation is wholly different. The overall aims of the Trust remain; to protect, record, and study the species and their habitats which are of conservation importance in Dorset. This includes not only plants and animals but features of geological, archaeological, scientific interest or of natural beauty. What is different today is the way in which we interpret these aims and go about achieving them.

As we have already seen, the main focus in the Trust's early years was the setting up of nature reserves. A second priority was the wish to influence policy and decision-making affecting the Dorset countryside. The expansion of the urban areas, the building of roads and a host of other planning issues were challenged by the Trust; as were the intensification of agriculture and the use of harmful sprays and fertilisers.

The Trust was a small organisation, initially with only 306 members. There were no permanent staff and no headquarters or conservation centres; its achievements were entirely due to the work done by volunteers. Yet its influence in these years was out of all proportion to its size.

Today the picture is very different. The Trust is a powerful organisation within the county

The view from north of Beaminster, where the 'Pastures New' project has been giving practical support to landowners and farmers in the restoration of ancient meadows.

ABOVE The staff of the Dorset Wildlife Trust, photographed at Brooklands Farm in March 2011.
BELOW The reserves, as here at Kingcombe Meadows, are open for the enjoyment and interest of both members of the Trust and the general public.

with some 25,000 members, an annual turnover of almost £4 million, and an establishment of over 80 professional conservationists and support staff. Besides the headquarters, there are six other conservation centres within the county, a network of 42 nature reserves covering 1300 hectares and about 1200 volunteers. What has happened in Dorset very much follows the national trends over the same time. The umbrella organisation for the 47 county naturalists' trusts, the Royal Society of Wildlife Trusts, represents some 800,000 members, has some 2,300 nature reserves covering 90,000 hectares and a volunteer force of 35,000.

Until recently, the underlying principle throughout the Trust's history has been to achieve conservation through the ownership and management of protected sites – nature reserves. These reserves enabled conservationists to be in control. However, they were like islands set in inhospitable surroundings and they were managed in isolation from each another.

Gradually, an alternative view began to take hold. Interestingly, some of the seeds of this idea originated from research into fragmented habitats on the Dorset heathlands. These heathlands are a patchwork set in surroundings of different types – woodland, plantations, grassland, farmland and urban areas. It was evident from studying the types and number of plants and animals which occurred on each of them that a key factor was the nature of the intervening areas rather than the quality of each part of the patchwork.

Related to this was the realisation that most

of the communities we wished to conserve had been highly influenced by human activity. In most cases, such as downland and heathland, they had been produced by the ways in which the land was farmed, they were not natural. People had been an essential component in these systems and this led to the concept of the 'living landscape'.

Reserves were still important as reservoir areas, but the intervening spaces ought to be managed in a way that improved the survival of species moving within the landscape. Man-made features such as gardens, churchyards and parks could also play a part. Added to this was the potential to restore areas to enhance their wildlife and to reduce the fragmentation of their habitats. Methods to achieve this had been

Dorset's butterflies include (*top left*) the green-veined white (seen mating), (*top right*) the marsh fritillary on a heath spotted orchid, (*above*) the marbled white on greater knapweed, and (*left*) the ringlet.

One of the Trust's Community projects gives wildlife friendly garden awards.

developed by ecologists during the latter part of the twentieth century, but the idea of ecological restoration had not originally been welcomed by conservationists. The concept of the 'living landscape' was rapidly and keenly taken up by the Wildlife Trusts as a flagship policy, although some other conservation agencies remained less enthusiastic.

In Dorset the concept seemed entirely appropriate as a way forward. To achieve this the old structure of the Trust, in which staff were grouped according to their speciality, was abandoned and the Trust was reorganised into three 'living landscape' teams; West Dorset, Mid Dorset, East and Urban Dorset, and a Living Seas team. Administration and finance

Alderholt churchyard has won the top 'Living Churchyard' award for introducing wildlife friendly management several times.

and some other functions remained countywide and operated from the headquarters. This new structure enables the Trust to promote the 'living landscape' concept more effectively.

The Trust will continue to do what it has always done in acquiring reserves and managing them and in resisting wholesale urban expansion and development in the countryside. However, in recent years a number of related factors have risen to the fore, such as climate change, sustainability, economic changes and changes in peoples' attitudes and perception. The concept of the 'living landscape' provides a much more useful model to address these issues. If this were achieved nationally the effect would be considerable. Disconnected areas of woodland, downland, heath, meadows and marshes would be linked up by restoring the areas between them and making towns and villages more amenable to wildlife. This would create an environment which people would value, be part of, and seek to maintain. When one looks at the map of areas within Dorset which are already subject to some form of conservation then one can see how easily these links can be established and how widespread is the current reach of the Trust.

One of the key features of the new approach is engaging with people and with communities much more than has been the case in the past. It seeks to encourage people to value and to appreciate the wildlife and landscape around

them and to broaden the constituency of support for wildlife. Increasingly there is engagement with people through activities such as the Living Churchyards Competition; the Wildlife Friendly Garden scheme and competition; educational activities with schools and colleges; promoting green spaces within the urban areas; and working with disadvantaged groups and other social groups.

The Living Churchyards Competition has operated for over 20 years and in that time has engaged with over 100 parishes throughout Dorset. Not only does it encourage local people to maintain their churchyards for the benefit of wildlife but it has provided an advice service to make this possible. Similarly the Wildlife Friendly Gardens Scheme, begun in 2009, has been widely supported with over 100 gardens being awarded a plaque recognising them as wildlife friendly. The first completion run in conjunction with this scheme in 2010 attracted over 50 entrants.

Roadside verges, like this one in the Blackmore Vale, are rich in flowers.

For many years the Trust has surveyed and noted important road verges mostly as sites for rare plants. It has been able to engage with the engineers who maintain the roadsides to ensure that cutting and maintenance is carried out with the least effect on the flora. Over the years a strong and healthy dialogue has been maintained which has benefited the plants and maintained linkages within the landscape.

As long ago as the late 1980s the Trust began to identify sites of nature conservation interest. These were often smaller sites which did not reach the standard of the statutorily notified sites but which were nevertheless important in a local context for their biodiversity. The listing of these sites was with the full cooperation of the landowners, who in most instances were proud of the fact that there were locations of considerable conservation value on their land. Together with

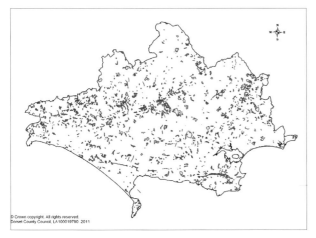

A map showing the location of Sites of Nature Conservation Interest in Dorset.

the listing came the opportunity to receive advice on the best way to manage these sites for their wildlife. This served two functions, it enabled the Trust to engage much more with people and it created a network in the landscape which supported wildlife. This network supplemented those provided by nature reserves and Sites of Special Scientific Interest. As the concept of the 'living landscape' developed it became clear that this network of conservation sites of differing status could provide the framework needed. All that was required was to strengthen the framework and add to it where there were gaps.

For many years, in collaboration with the Farming and Wildlife Advisory Group, the Trust has provided an advice service to farmers. The most recent Stewardship Schemes are particularly important. The Sites of Nature Conservation Interest (SNCI) project, in the early 1990s, had identified most of the remaining 3% of the pre war total of old meadows and pastures which had survived wartime and post wartime ploughing. The Trust took a major step forward in 1996 when their Farming Liaison Officer, Jeremy Powne, and FWAG's adviser, John Sheaves, attended a Ministry of Agriculture meeting in 1996 to discuss the Countryside Stewardship scheme, then still in its early days.

Conservation bodies had been campaigning for an option within the scheme to pay farmers for preserving and enhancing rapidly disappearing hay meadows and pastures. The Ministry was afraid that not many people would apply for such an option and did not wish to include it unless they could be sure of a sufficient response. Asked who would 'deliver' such an option both Jeremy and John said 'we will', thus committing their organisations to a path which was to have considerable influence with farmers and landowners.

Persuading farmers to adopt these options within a wider countryside preservation scheme became the principal focus. From this sprang the Pastures New project; an important initiative in west Dorset. This recognised that farmers needed help if a wildlife rich landscape was to be achieved. The project provided management advice to landowners, assisted with seeking capital funding, provided a machinery ring and provided a grazing brokerage scheme and importantly volunteer labour. Areas of grassland were restored by seeding techniques developed in restoration ecology designed to create species

ABOVE The Lorton 'Green valley' with Lorton Meadows nature reserve in the foreground leading down to the RSPB Lodmoor nature reserve and Weymouth Bay.
RIGHT Restoring the course of the South Winterborne chalk stream near Winterborne Herringston as part of the 'wild rivers' project.

rich meadows.

The success of this project has led to further ones within the Pastures New Scheme. Farmers and landowners with smaller holdings have been enabled to protect and enhance unimproved grassland fragments, hedgerows, ponds, flushes, and streamside woodlands by taking advantage of government grants. Under this programme the Trust has been able to ensure that for the next 10 years 609 hectares of land on 11 separate holdings is managed with conservation at the fore.

The Trust has itself moved out into the county with the opening over the last decade of its Conservation Centres. There are now seven. The Urban Wildlife Centre at Upton has engaged with the urban communities of Poole and Bournemouth; particularly with young people and disadvantaged groups. It has also begun to

Some of Dorset's orchids:

OPPOSITE PAGE: *Top left* common spotted orchid, *Top centre* bog orchid, *Top right* greater butterfly orchid, *Bottom left* southern marsh orchid, *Bottom right* heath spotted orchid.

THIS PAGE: *Top left* frog orchid, *Top centre* fragrant orchid, *Top right* autumn lady's tresses, *Below left* bee orchid, *Below right* green winged orchid.

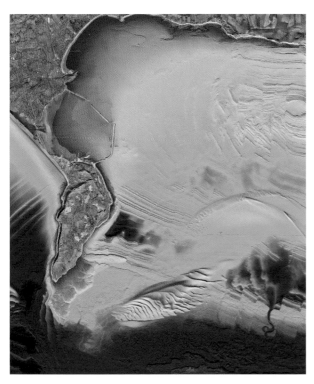

Map of the sea bed in Weymouth Bay produced during DORIS (DORset Integrated Seabed Survey) which has provided data on the topography, substrates and biodiversity of the Dorset coastal waters. A collaborative project involving DWT, Maritime and Coastguard Agency, Channel Coastal Observatory and the Royal Navy, with funding from Viridor Credits Environmental Co., Natural England, Dorset Strategic Partnership, University of Southampton and National Oceanography Centre.

Trustees and staff discuss the 'living landscape' work with the Chairman and Chief Executive of the Royal Society of Wildlife Trusts, Michael Allen and Stephanie Hilborne.

promote the benefits to health and well-being of a landscape rich in wildlife. Similar engagement with the local community occurs at the centre at Lorton. The Trust in collaboration with other conservation agencies has secured the Lorton Valley as a 'green lung' for Weymouth and the Centre provides the ideal location to engage with the surrounding communities.

Since the 1970s the Trust has held a prominent position in marine and coastal conservation. Today this work has expanded. The Centre at Kimmeridge continues to provide an introduction to marine ecology. However, marine conservation has come to the fore nationally with the development of new legislation and the setting up of marine conservation zones. Thirty percent of the sea area out to six nautical miles has been selected as a Marine Special Area of Conservation.

The Trust in collaboration with the University of Southampton, the Maritime and Coastguard Agency, Channel Coastal Observatory and the Royal Navy, has elevated this topic to a new level, pioneering a sea bed mapping programme for the Dorset coastal waters. This advanced project has provided first-hand information on the structure and topography of the sea bed and has enabled the distribution of various habitats and species to be mapped. For the first time marine conservationists have had the type of information that has long been familiar to terrestrial ecologists; it will enable significant decisions to be made over what to protect.

Finally, the Trust continues to comment on policy. This it can do on local issues by raising matters directly with councillors or local authorities, as well as with Members of Parliament. At a national level the Trust contributes to policy issues raised by the Government through the umbrella body for county trusts, the Royal Society of Wildlife Trusts.

Recently, the Trust prepared a series of questions on conservation and the environmental

An artist's impression on the new Chesil Centre.

issues, which it placed before all the candidates in Dorset standing in the 2010 General Election and published the responses. As part of a national initiative from RSWT the Trust has produced narratives for each of the parliamentary constituencies in Dorset describing the key wildlife features of each constituency and their needs, and these have been circulated to Members of Parliament and other representatives.

After 50 years the work of the Trust remains faithful to that envisaged by its founders. It actively promotes conservation on the ground and seeks to influence decision makers. Many of the issues affecting wildlife have changed, and we are now concerned with issues such as climate change and sustainability. The membership remains as actively concerned as ever about its environment and Dorset's wildlife. We must continue to protect what we have, to be more influential, to engage with a more diverse number of people making them aware of wildlife, to continue to increase our membership, but above all to lead and inspire, and to uphold the vision held fifty years ago by the founders of the Dorset Wildlife Trust.

Dorset Wildlife Trust Nature Reserves

ASHLEY WOOD

12 hectares. Originally part of a large woodland area, an ancient hazel & ash coppice with a display of bluebells & wood anemones in early spring. Rotational coppicing and mown rides create open areas encouraging butterflies & wild flowers.

Wildlife interest: Excellent variety of woodland birds & flowers, with orpine & early purple orchid along the rides; great spotted woodpeckers nest. Silver-washed fritillary & speckled wood butterflies can be seen in the cleared glades.

Best time to visit: Any time of year but come in early spring for a show of bluebells.
Access: Limited due to the wet nature of the ground.
Location: Map ref: ST 928048 From Blandford travel south on the B3082. Approximately 500m past garage on left there is a track, next to a house, into the reserve. Access is by foot only through the field gate. Parking not available on site.

Wood anemones carpet a ride at Ashley Wood.

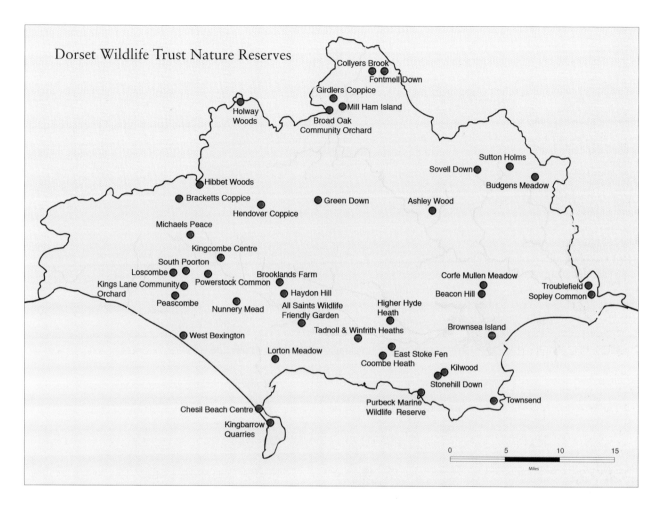

Dorset Wildlife Trust Nature Reserves

Collyers Brook
Fontmell Down
Girdlers Coppice
Mill Ham Island
Holway Woods
Broad Oak Community Orchard
Sutton Holms
Sovell Down
Budgens Meadow
Hibbet Woods
Bracketts Coppice
Green Down
Ashley Wood
Hendover Coppice
Michaels Peace
Kingcombe Centre
South Poorton
Loscombe
Brooklands Farm
Corfe Mullen Meadow
Troublefield
Kings Lane Community Orchard
Powerstock Common
Beacon Hill
Sopley Common
Peascombe
Haydon Hill
Nunnery Mead
All Saints Wildlife Friendly Garden
Higher Hyde Heath
Brownsea Island
West Bexington
Tadnoll & Winfrith Heaths
Lorton Meadow
East Stoke Fen
Coombe Heath
Kilwood
Stonehill Down
Townsend
Chesil Beach Centre
Purbeck Marine Wildlife Reserve
Kingbarrow Quarries

0   5   10   15
Miles

BEACON HILL

The Urban Wildlife Centre is at Beacon Hill just outside Corfe Mullen, on the edge of Upton Heath. The Centre provides a base for the East Dorset & Urban team. The Centre is a focus for DWT's work in the urban area & an education centre for school & group visits. A small demonstration wildlife garden lies next to the building.

Visits by appointment, tel. 01202 692033.

Location: Map ref SY 976949. The Urban Wildlife Centre lies at the top of Beacon Hill Lane, off the Old Wareham Road, south west of Corfe Mullen.

The meeting room at Beacon Hill Urban Wildlife Centre.

BRACKETTS COPPICE

38 hectares. A quiet & secret ancient woodland slopes down to a small fast-flowing stream. Swathes of wood anemones, with orchids providing colour to the open areas. The haymeadows are cut annually & wood pasture is grazed, creating fields of wild flowers & butterflies.

Wildlife interest: Typical woodland bird species are found, the stream providing sightings of grey wagtails & kingfishers. Flowers include early purple orchids, sanicle & dog violets, with betony, fleabane & devil's-bit scabious in the grassland. Butterflies include silver-washed & marsh fritillaries. Autumn brings an abundance of fungi.

Best time to visit: Spring for the flowers & birds, summer for butterflies.

Access: Limited parking with difficult access due to steep and muddy tracks.

Location: Map ref: ST 514074. Gate entrance & small car park on S. side of minor road, 2 miles due north of Corscombe & 3 miles west of Halstock.

ABOVE Headland Common at Bracketts Coppice.
BELOW Apple Day at Broad Oak Community Orchard.

BROAD OAK COMMUNITY ORCHARD

0.18 hectares. Orchards, once widespread in the south-west, are now few. Given to the Trust in 1979 & managed by a group of local villagers.

Wildlife interest: Common fruit tree varieties & old rarities such as Autumn Pearmain & King George V. The unimproved grassland supports many wild flowers such as ox-eye daisy, devil's-bit scabious & corky-fruited water-dropwort & also butterflies.

Best time to visit: After the winter months. An annual 'Open Day' is held in early October.
Access: Fairly good, with rough-mown paths, but on-site parking is limited.
Location: Map ref: ST 791124 Turn south off the A357 at Sturminster Newton, just east of the River Stour bridge/traffic lights at The Bull pub on to a minor road. Through the village of Broad Oak (1 mile) & the orchard is on the left just before a sharp bend.

BROOKLANDS FARM CONSERVATION CENTRE

Site of the DWT's headquarters in the River Cerne valley, a few miles north of Dorchester. Chalk grassland, enclosed by hedgerows, has been developed as a hay meadow, now colonised by typical Dorset downland flowers. A pond was excavated in 1996 &, apart from the introduction of a few plants, allowed to develop naturally.
Wildlife interest: The hay meadow was created by spreading cut material from a local reserve & cowslip, yellow rattle & kidney vetch now thrive, with thyme on the shallow soil 'lynchets'. In summer the pond is full of water beetles, dragon-flies & damselflies & butterflies over the field.

The conservation area at Brooklands Farm.

Best time to visit: Spring & summer. Any time of the year can produce an unexpected bird species, particularly at migration. Centre open during normal working hours.
Access: Easy access to most of the grounds & the building. Disabled toilet at the Centre.
Location: Map ref. SY 666952. On the west side of the A352 Dorchester to Cerne Abbas road, about 2 miles north of Charminster.

BROWNSEA ISLAND & VILLA WILDLIFE CENTRE

101 hectares. Diverse habitats & wildlife, including a red squirrel population. Reserve leased from the National Trust, situated in Poole Harbour with a large sheltered lagoon; particularly important for overwintering & summer breeding birds. A day spent exploring its flooded woodland, lakes, reedbed & pine woods is unlikely to disappoint.
Wildlife interest: Large flocks of waders, particularly avocets, black-tailed godwits & visiting wildfowl over winter. Replaced in the summer by breeding common and sandwich terns, gulls & little egrets. The reed beds & alder carr are home to water voles & sika deer, with kingfishers & water rails providing avian interest.
Best time to visit: Boats to the island from March

Brownsea Island. The view from the bird hide overlooking the inland lake.

to October. Come early in the year for winter bird visitors, or in summer for breeding terns. Autumn is best for red squirrel watching.
Access: Good viewing from hides, & a system of well-maintained paths & boardwalk give access to most of the habitat for all abilities. The Villa Visitor Centre provides displays and live camera links to the lagoon and red squirrels. Toilet available.
Location: Map ref. SZ 028878. No road access.

Devil's-bit scabious and fleabane at Bugdens Meadows.

Public ferries run daily to the island from Poole Quay and Sandbanks from 10am March – October. Check for details. Access to the reserve is 150m from the National Trust Quay on the island.

BUGDENS MEADOWS
2 hectares. Species-rich meadows at the heart of Verwood, in the east of the county; an oasis for the community and wildlife alike, in this busy town, protected on its southern side by a copse.
Wildlife interest: The meadowland includes devil's-bit scabious, spotted orchid, sneezewort and knapweed, all uncommon in Dorset and nationally.
Best time to visit: Spring and early summer.
Access: A gate from the Ringwood road, B3081, that runs through Verwood.
Location: Map ref. SU 089088. From the B3078 Wimborne to Cranborne road take the B3081 Ringwood road heading south east. Just after entering Three legged Cross, take a left at the 2nd roundabout to Verwood and on entering Verwood, the reserve will be seen on the right hand side, just before a chapel.

COLLYER'S BROOK
0.81 hectares. This reserve is a useful community facility in the north east of the county. It has linked spring-fed stew ponds, used for breeding fish in the Middle Ages, edged by wet woodland. Adjoining picnic site & hide provide good spots to view birds, dragonflies & bats which live in the area.
Wildlife interest: Little egrets, kingfishers & water rails inhabit the wet parts, feeding on a remnant population of trout & sticklebacks. Marsh tit & siskin amongst the trees. Otters visit the site & in summer evenings soprano pipistrelles & Daubenton's bats feed over the ponds. Marsh marigolds & yellow flag irises add colour.
Best time to visit: All-year round interest, but probably best in midsummer.

Access: Good access to viewing areas.
Location: Map ref: ST 870168. Leave the A350 at Fontmell Magna opposite the Crown Pub towards Ashmore. The reserve is approx. 1/4 mile on the right. Small car park adjoining.

COOMBE HEATH

41 hectares. This reserve is a surviving area of dry & wet heathland, home to rare reptiles, several species of butterfly & typical heathland birds. Evidence of its history is provided by two bowl barrows in the middle of the reserve.

Wildlife interest: Apart from dominant heather & ling, dodder and lousewort can be found on the heath, with yellow bartsia & spotted orchids in the cleared edges & bog asphodel in the wetter areas. Dartford warblers & stonechats can be found in the scrub, grayling, silver-studded blue, white admiral & silver-washed fritillary butterflies in the open & dragonflies & bog bush crickets around the bog pools.

ABOVE Collyer's Brook ponds.
BELOW Coombe Heath: boggy pool with rare heathland plants, including lesser bladderwort.

Best time to visit: Late summer for the heather colour.
Access: Uneven ground & often wet underfoot.

Corfe Mullen Meadows: hundreds of green-winged orchids.

Location: Map ref. SY 862848. Turn left after the station in Wool onto Bindon Lane. At the second junction turn right at Highwood. Park at end of tarmac road; walk down track into the reserve.

CORFE MULLEN MEADOWS
5 hectares. On the outskirts of Corfe Mullen. Managed traditionally as hay meadows supporting many wildflower species. Cut each year in July & grazed until the following February.
Wildlife interest: One of the largest populations of green-winged orchids in the county. Home to bird's-foot trefoil, black knapweed & yellow bartsia.
Best time to visit: May, for the meadow flowers.
Access: Good walking surface. Take care when

stock is on the reserve.
Location: Map ref. SY 980967. Travelling south on A350 (Blandford road, north), turn left at traffic lights for Corfe Mullen on the old Wareham road. Travel for 1.2km , turn left down Waterloo road for further 1.2km, reserve is on the right opposite houses.

DORCHESTER WILDLIFE GARDEN
This churchyard area has been developed as a community garden with the permission of West Dorset District Council and in cooperation with Dorset County Museum. It is dedicated to the memory of Alan Swindall, DWT chairman. Benches made by HMP: The Verne and wildlife friendly planting makes the area a welcome resting place in the centre of Dorchester for tourists and locals.
Wildlife Interest: Information on wildlife gardening and wildlife on your doorstep.

Dorchester Wildlife Meadow: the wildlife garden at St John's Church, managed in association with Dorset County Museum.

Goldcrest, blue tit, jackdaw, robin, blackbird, pigeon all nest in the garden and a peregrine can sometimes be seen using the church spire as a look-out. 6 bat species have been recorded feeding over the garden.

Best time to visit:
Planting provides interest throughout the year and the annual meadow is particularly attractive in June/July

Access: Gate and steps from Church Street and disabled access from High East Street.

Location: Map ref. SY 694907. Behind All Saints Church (decommissioned), High East Street, Dorchester (opp. The King's Arms)

EAST STOKE FEN

4.5 hectares. Lies to the east of Wool in the River Frome floodplain. The terrain, ranges from reedmarsh, wet woodland to oak copse. Reed fen is a declining habitat in the county, but one which has provided much information on the history of vegetation changes.

Wildlife interest: Common reed dominates the reedbeds, providing good reed warbler territory.

Best time to visit: Spring for the bluebells & early summer.

Access: Limited footpath access & very wet all year.

Location: Map ref. SY 864865. In Wool turn left after the station onto Bindon Lane. Drive past Bindon Farm on the bend, & access to the reserve is a mile further on the left via a public footpath.

FONTMELL DOWN

60 hectares. High on a steeply sloping area of the North Dorset Downs, this reserve has far-reaching views across the Blackmore Vale. Interspersed scrub & woodland provide shelter for many species of butterfly, while the open chalk grassland of the lower slopes is covered in wildflowers in the spring & summer months.

Wildlife interest: Numerous wild flower species can be found including many different orchids & the rare early gentian. Many butterflies are seen on the southern slopes including Adonis & chalkhill blues & silver spotted skippers. Skylarks

East Stoke Fen at a remote stretch of the River Frome.

Girdlers Coppice borders the River Stour.

ABOVE Fontmell Down: Adonis blue butterflies feeding on cow dung.
BELOW Cowslips on Littledown at Fontmell Down in April.

often sing above.
Best time to visit: Spring & early summer
Access: Steep slopes in some parts.
Location: Map ref: ST 887176. Access from the C13 top road between Shaftesbury & Blandford, opposite Compton Abbas airfield. Parking at the National Trust car park at the top of Spread Eagle Hill.

GIRDLERS COPPICE

7 hectares. This centuries-old area of ancient oak woodland & hazel coppice slopes down to flood meadows by the River Stour. Much is still traditionally managed in a coppice rotation. Rich ground flora in summer, attracts many butterfly species.
NB – dogs not allowed in this reserve.
Wildlife interest: Amongst oak, & ash is the rare wild service. Spring migrants include willow warblers, blackcaps & spotted flycatchers. The colourful woodland floor includes creeping jenny, bugle, devil's-bit scabious & saw wort & in some shady areas violet helleborine. The nearby River Stour brings dragonfly & damselfly species in summer.
Best time to visit: Spring & summer for the flowers.

Access: Steep slopes in the wood & wet ground conditions in the fields near the river.

Location: Map ref. ST 800135. Access from the car park for Fiddleford Manor, situated on the north side of the A357 about 2 miles east of Sturminster Newton.

GREENHILL DOWN

12 hectares. Chalk downland, unimproved scrubby pasture, restored dewpond, veteran trees & coppice woodland.

Wildlife interest: Trees provide shelter for 5 tit species. Woodland bird species include nuthatch & treecreeper, with blackcap, garden & willow warblers amongst the summer migrants. Dragon & damselfly species inhabit the pond. The downland is good for butterflies. Wildflowers include woodsage, gorse & foxglove; rock rose & pyramidal orchid appear on the chalk slopes, & marjoram & toothwort are found in the woods.

Best time to visit: Any time, but come in summer for the display of flowers.

Access: Limited paths with rough & steep terrain.

Location: Map ref. ST 789038. Leave A354 at Milborne St. Andrew & follow signs for Milton Abbas, then Hilton. Park in Hilton village, please do not obstruct the church. Walk up road, for about 1 mile, directly opposite church; this then becomes a bridleway.

HAYDON HILL

10 hectares. A stroll from the Trust's Brooklands Farm base, this reserve is on a steep north-facing slope of unimproved chalk grassland in the River Cerne valley. It supports a diverse range of flowers, birds & butterflies.

Wildlife interest: Yellowhammer & linnet in hedgerows & field margins. Barn owl, kestrel & buzzards prey on the numerous voles & shrews. Red clover, autumn gentian squinancywort & harebell grow on the easterly field, with common blue, green hairstreak, marbled white & orange tip among the butterflies found.

Greenhill Down in the autumn.

Best time to visit: Summer for the flowers & butterflies.

Access: Steeply sloping ground on most of the reserve.

Location: Map ref. SY 671945. Two miles north of Charminster on the west side of the A352 Dorchester to Cerne Abbas road. Look for a small pull-off car parking area at the foot of the hill.

Haydon Hill with Brooklands Farm, Dorset Wildlife Trust HQ in the distance.

Hendover Coppice: fly orchid.

HENDOVER COPPICE

12.11 hectares. Peaceful woodland site used as a place for reflection by monks from the nearby Hillfield Friary. Subsequent commercial crop of conifers was cleared by the last owner, allowing native species, mostly ash with a hazel understorey, to regenerate. Donated to DWT in 2005, this is an area with fantastic flora and good views to Somerset.

Wildlife interest: Willow warbler & black cap in spring. Many wild flowers can be found here. Dormice have also been seen.

Best time to visit: Any time.

Access: Uneven paths with numerous tree stumps on steeply sloping ground.

Location: Map ref. ST 634038. The reserve lies to the north of the road between Minterne Magna and Holywell (Evershot). The gated entrance is close to the public viewpoint at Highfield Hill, just W. of the minor road leading steeply downhill to Hillfield Friary. Parking available at the nearby D.C.C. Hillfield car park.

HIBBITTS WOODS

9.34 hectares. Two attractive areas of ancient woodland, including a small flower-rich meadow at Adam's Green, just east of Halstock, in north-east Dorset.

Wildlife Interest: The species in the meadow include devil's-bit scabious, black knapweed and common fleabane; the two rich woodland areas, with bluebells, include, to the north, broad-leaved woodland with bird's-nest and early purple orchid, wild daffodil and wood anemone; in the semi-natural deciduous southern area are found yellow archangel, goldilocks buttercup and town-hall clock.

Best time to visit: Spring for the woodlands and summer for the meadowland.

Access: Lane side parking. Damp conditions underfoot with gently sloping ground.

Location: Map ref. ST 546075. The hamlet of Adam's Green, near Halstock, is 7 miles south

ABOVE Deep gullies occur in the northern Hibbitts Woods.
RIGHT The entrance to southern part of Hibbitts Woods
with false oxlip in the foreground.

of Yeovil. From Yeovil take the A37 south; turn
off onto a B road passing to the west of Sutton
Bingham Reservoir. At Halstock turn left to
Adam's Green, ½ mile to the east. Park at the end
of the village and finger posts indicate the two
woodland areas to the north and south of the
road.

HIGHER HYDE HEATH

54 hectares. An internationally important area of
dry & wet lowland heathland & woodland.
Wildlife interest: The heather, ling & gorse
provide shelter for resident stonechats & Dartford
warblers. Emperor moths & silver-studded

blue butterflies, as well as sand lizards & other reptiles. In summer migrant nightjars are found on the heath, with hobbies feeding over the peaty pools on the various damsel & dragonflies. Interesting plants include insectivorous sundews, pale butterwort & early marsh orchids. A bird hide overlooks a pond.

Best time to visit: All year round interest. Late spring & summer for butterflies, dragonflies & migrant birds. Colourful in late summer when the heather flowers.

Access: Several paths & a marked trail cross the heath. Disabled access to the bird hide & viewing area.

Location: Map ref. SY 854899. Lies to the north-east side of the Puddletown Road, between Bovington & Wareham. Small car park just west of the approach road to the golf club, tucked away behind a group of single-storey industrial buildings at Hanson Yard.

HOLWAY WOODS

16 hectares. Sits high with superb views of S. Somerset. Mixture of mature woodland with a good variety of birds, plants, butterflies & mammals.

Wildlife interest: Tawny owls, song thrushes & other woodland bird species, with spotted flycatchers & willow warblers in summer. Large mammals include roe deer & badgers. Springtime show of bluebells, primroses & pink purslane.

Best time to visit: Late spring & early summer.

Access: Limited due to the steep terrain.

Mixed broad-leaved woodland in Holway Woods.

Location: Map ref. ST 633204. Take the B3145 Charlton Horethorne/Wincanton road north of Sherborne. After 2 miles fork left at a red finger post then turn left soon afterwards down a narrow lane. The reserve is ½ mile down on both sides of the road. Parking is in a small old quarry on the right at the top of the hill or a lay-by on the left at the bottom of the hill.

KILWOOD

16 hectares. Once an area of clay mining, dating back to Roman times, this reserve has been allowed to regenerate naturally after extraction stopped in the 1970s. The result is a birch & oak woodland, a number of deep ponds & grassland.
Wildlife interest: Dormice & deer live in the woods, along with typical woodland birds & the less commonly seen woodcock, goldcrests

ABOVE Kilwood from Corfe Ridge, with Poole Harbour in the background.
BELOW Kilwood: wood sorrel growing on fallen oak log.

& marsh tits. Flower species are varied, with moschatel in the woods, yellow iris in the reeds & heath spotted orchids & devil's-bit scabious in the grassland. Numerous insect species thrive, such as meadow & field grasshoppers, along with speckled wood, painted lady & small copper butterflies. 15 species of dragonflies have been recorded around the ponds.

Best time to visit: Spring & summer.

Access: The 150m track into the reserve has a good surface otherwise conditions underfoot are uneven & damp.

Location: Map ref. SY 933825. Turn off the A351 roundabout at Stoborough Green, take the road to the Blue Pool. The reserve entrance is on the left just after the junction to East Creech on the right hand side.

KING BARROW QUARRIES

12.22 hectares. Site of former stone quarries abandoned 100 years ago. It has been left to regenerate naturally, although there is some scrub management & control of recreational activities. High on Portland, the reserve has excellent views of the Dorset mainland, Chesil Beach & the Fleet lagoon.

Wildlife interest: Interesting plant species include horseshoe vetch, kidney vetch and autumn gentian. Lichens & bryophytes are plentiful. Adonis & chalkhill blue butterflies can be seen. Bird species include whitethroats, linnets, meadow pipits & little owls.

Best time: Late spring & summer.

King Barrow Quarries, Portland.

ABOVE Lousewort in Yonder Cowlease, Kingcombe
Meadows.
ABOVE LEFT Kingcombe Meadows: early purple orchids.
BELOW Kingcombe: Mary's Well Lane in the autumn.

Access: Plenty of paths but sheer rock faces, steep slopes & loose stones underfoot.
Location: Map ref. SY 690728. On the Isle of Portland take the A354, climb the hill & immediately look for small parking area set back off the east side of the road. Entrance to the reserve is marked by a finger post just off Yeates road.

KINGCOMBE MEADOWS & THE KINGCOMBE CENTRE

185 hectares. A visit to **Kingcombe Meadows** is a step back in time. Reserve is still managed as a working farm, grazed by cows & sheep, using traditional methods without artificial fertilisers or pesticides. The result is a patchwork of fields & unimproved grassland, broken up by thick hedges, streams, ponds, ancient green lanes & wooded areas alongside the River Hooke. **The Kingcombe Centre** offers courses, walks, events & a café that serves light lunches & refreshments – to check café opening times & course details tel: 01300 320684 or www.kingcombe.org. You can also stay at the Centre regardless of whether you are a course participant or not.

Wildlife interest: Typical wildflowers in woodland & marshy areas. The grassy meadows sustain many common species, & also lady's mantle, corky-fruited water dropwort, pepper saxifrage, devil's-bit scabious & knapweed. Butterflies include varieties of skipper & fritillaries. Birds abound, with visiting summer warblers, as well as dippers & grey wagtails.

Best time to visit: Any time of the year; particularly impressive in spring/early summer for the blaze of colour, the insects, birds & butterflies.

Access: Limited tracks across the meadows. Visitor Centre.

Location: Map ref. SY 554990. From Dorchester take the A37 to Yeovil. Just after the village of Grimstone turn left on A356. Continue past Maiden Newton & turn left at the top of the hill to Toller Porcorum. Turn right in the village

King's Lane Community Orchard, Powerstock.

signposted to Lower Kingcombe. Travel 1 mile, look for Kingcombe Visitors Centre sign on right.

KING'S LANE COMMUNITY ORCHARD

0.317 hectares. Remnant of the old cider apple orchards which formerly surrounded Powerstock village.

Wildlife Interest: Very old apple trees in various states of decay, which is excellent for invertebrates. The grassland, which is grazed briefly by sheep each year, supports a wide variety of spring and late summer flowers including many wet land species such as marsh marigold, ragged robin, moschatel and opposite-leaved golden saxifrage, many butterflies and other insects. A stream marks the southern border with banks covered in Pellia liverworts.

Best time to visit: spring for the apple blossom and early flowers.

Access: Fairly good but sloping and boggy at the bottom near the stream. **No Parking on the site.** Park near The Three Horseshoes pub in Powerstock village and walk down the lane.

Location: Map ref: SY 518960 to east of centre of Powerstock village 500m below The Horseshoes Pub on King's Lane Eggardon Hill. The orchard is entered through a small gate east of Hillside Cottage.

LORTON MEADOWS & CONSERVATION CENTRE

34 hectares. Situated on the edge of the urban sprawl of Weymouth, this is an area of unimproved grassland with views over Portland & Weymouth Harbour. The nature reserve is open all year. To find out the opening times of the Wildlife Centre please call 01305 816456. Displays, small shop & toilets with picnic area & parking (disabled facilities).

Wildlife Interest: The grassland attracts a variety of butterfly species, including marbled white, common and holly blues & small & large skipper. The proximity of the RSPB reserves at Lodmoor & Radipole may account for a variety of migrant birds, particularly warblers, with barn owls & Cetti's warblers among the resident species.

Best time: Spring & summer.

Access: Network of paths across the reserve.

Location: Map ref. SY 674827. Take A354 Dorchester to Weymouth road. Turn left at Lorton Lane, just past the Littlemoor road traffic lights. Continue to end of lane.

ABOVE Lorton Meadows: grass vetchling.
BELOW Woodland pasture at Lorton Meadows.

LOSCOMBE

10 hectares. Fields intersected by ancient hedgerows, sloping steeply down to a small stream & marshy ground. Mostly unimproved grassland. Old sunken lane at the top of the reserve.

Wildlife interest: Small colony of snake's head fritillaries amongst other grassland species. Wetter areas support a wide variety of plants including southern marsh orchids. To the east of the reserve, numerous yellow meadow ant hills cover the steep slopes.

Best time to visit: Spring & summer for wildflowers & butterflies. Winter for siskins, redpolls, fieldfares & redwings.

Access: Not easy due to the boggy ground adjacent to the stream & the steepness of the fields.

Location: Map ref. SY 502979. Just north of Bridport, turn east off the A3066 (Beaminster road) towards Mangerton, head for Powerstck & turn north over the river bridge into West Milton village. Keep left & first right to Loscombe, bearing right in the village. The reserve gate entrance & car park is on the right opposite a line of cottages.

Ancient ant hills are a feature of the steep slopes at Loscombe.

MICHAEL'S PEACE

4.5 hectares. Large pond & reedbed fed by a small stream, surrounded by wet woodland & boggy grassland below the spring line.

Wildlife interest: A range of woodland plant species, including primroses & opposite-leaved golden-saxifrage. The grassland has meadowsweet & marsh valerian. Migrant summer warblers. The reedbeds provide shelter for resident species with an occasional egret or wintering wildfowl.

The pond in winter at Michael's Peace.

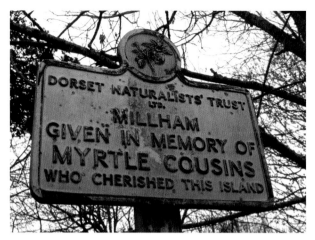

The old notice on Mill Ham Island on the River Stour of the memorial gift of the reserve.

Best time to visit: Spring & summer.
Access: Some tracks but generally difficult underfoot due to the very boggy ground.
Location: Map ref. ST 522009. Turn south off A356 onto the B3163. Turn left to Hooke then first left into narrow lane for Toller Whelme. Very limited parking/turning.

MILL HAM ISLAND

0.8 hectares. Cross the fields & over a small bridge to find this small reserve, with steep banks to River Stour on one side & a wet reedy area to the other on the river's old course. With its dense vegetation, this little visited area offers a retreat for water birds.

Wildlife interest: Swans, moorhens & ducks with herons & reed buntings in the reeds & goldfinches feeding on teasels. Naturally occurring scrubby plants, including comfrey. Various tree species planted 25 years ago.

Best time to visit: Any, but avoid times of heavy rain & high water levels.

Access: Very overgrown without paths.

Location: Map ref. ST 824126. 4 miles west of Sturminster Newton, turn east off A357 signposted to Child Okeford & park by the railway bridge. Take the public footpath across the fields to the river & reserve entrance.

Nunnery Mead.

NUNNERY MEAD

6 hectares. Lowland area of former water meadows, with small area of woodland & site of a Roman Villa/temple & medieval village. Water from the River Frome is diverted to flood the fields using restored Victorian sluices.

Wildlife interest: Kingfisher, dipper & grey wagtail. Potential for visiting winter birds & migrating waders. Signs of otters & water voles. Pignut & bird's-foot trefoil in the drier parts, with eyebright on the ground previously disturbed by archaeological digging.

Best time to visit: Any, but visitors braving wet conditions may be rewarded by sightings of birds.

Access: Limited by difficult ground conditions & no parking close by.

Location: Map ref. SY 615953. Turn left off A37 (Dorchester to Yeovil road) just past Grimstone, on to A356. Turn left in Frampton at sign to Southover. Limited parking along roadside. Reserve reached by foot only or bicycle from here. Follow road round to the right through Southover until end of houses. Take the path/cycleway to reach the entrance (approx. 500m) to the reserve on your right marked with information panel.

Peascombe, with the strip lynchets at Loders visible in the background.

PEASCOMBE

3 hectares. In a quiet corner of West Dorset, this reserve is set on a hillside adjoining the village of Loders. A grazed meadow slopes down to woodland alongside the River Aske.

Wildlife interest: Typical woodland plant species such as opposite-leaved golden-saxifrage: black knapweed, common bird's-foot trefoil & ragged robin found in the grassland. Dormice have been found nesting in the hedgerows. Community orchard.

Best time to visit: Spring & early summer. The reserve gets very wet & boggy in winter.

Access: Very limited due to the sloping ground & wet conditions underfoot.

Location: Map ref. SY 498944. Park at east end of the village of Loders, found on a minor road running parallel to and north of the A35, about 3 miles east of Bridport. The reserve is a short distance on the right up and along a narrow lane heading north, just past a small graveyard.

POWERSTOCK COMMON

115 hectares. Superb views of Dorset's coastline. Range of habitats, chiefly woodland, but with open grassy areas along the line of the disused railway, with hedgebanks & numerous small ponds. Range of wildlife & flowers; particularly important for butterfly species.

Wildlife interest: Resident woodland bird species, together with a number of migrants such as willow warblers & chiffchaffs. Wildflowers include bluebells, pendulous sedge, bee orchid, rock rose, dyers greenweed & devil's-bit scabious. Speckled wood & wood white, marsh fritillary & brown argus butterflies. Superb for newts & dragonflies in the ponds.

Best time to visit: Interest at any time, but best in spring & early summer.

Access: Generally good with wide clear paths.

Location: Map ref. SY 547974. Situated about 3 miles west of Maiden Newton, the Reserve entrance/parking area lies adjacent to a disused railway bridge on a minor road parallel to & about a mile west of the A356, connecting the B3163 with the A35.

Powerstock Common in spring.

A colourful display of bogbean on one of the ponds at Powerstock Common.

PURBECK MARINE WILDLIFE RESERVE & FINE FOUNDATION MARINE CENTRE

3,500 hectares. Extending along a beautiful stretch of Dorset's Jurassic Coast, with splendid views from grassy cliff tops & underwater nature trails for divers & snorkellers, this nationally important reserve is best accessed from Kimmeridge Bay. **The Fine Foundation Marine Centre**, with interactive displays & aquaria, provides a fascinating & vital source of information, encouraging all ages to explore the bay, its ledges & rockpools.

Wildlife interest: Wide variety of seaweeds & rockpool life such as sea anemones, crabs, fish & invertebrates. The Marine Centre's live underwater camera provides a window beneath the sea for those who like to stay dry, while the snorkelling trail guides the more adventurous

ABOVE Low tide at Kimmeridge Bay.
BELOW The Fine Foundation Marine Centre, Kimmeridge.

Rock samphire, one of the shore plants in Kimmeridge Bay.

rockpools slippery & uneven. The Marine Centre is very user-friendly.

Location: Map ref. SY 909789. Take the A351 from Wareham to Corfe Castle & the first turn right to Creech. Follow road to the top of a steep hill & round a hairbend bend signposted to Church Knowle. Approx. 2 miles on, turn right to Kimmeridge. Drive through village to toll booth. Parking fee payable.

through different seabed habitats where species such as ballan wrasse, mullet, lobster & tompot blennies can be seen against a colourful backdrop of rainbow wrack & coraline seaweeds.

Best time to visit: Limited access in winter. A summer day spent at Kimmeridge is a wonderful outing. Check tide times to gain the most reward.

Access: Cliff paths are steep in places, the

SOPLEY COMMON

33 hectares. Sopley has both dry & wet heath, bordered by woodland. Late summer colours of dwarf gorse & heather.

Wildlife interest: The dry heathland, covered with ling & bell heather, is home to sand lizards & smooth snakes, with heath grasshoppers, wood tiger beetle & grayling butterfly. In the moss-covered boggy areas are cotton grass, round & long-leaved sundews & bog asphodel. Many dragonfly & damsel species share the habitat with raft spiders & bog bush crickets.

Sopley Common.

Best time to visit: High summer for the wildlife, autumn for the colour.
Access: Soft & uneven ground conditions.
Location: Map ref. SZ 129971. From Hurn bridge roundabout travel 300m along Avon Causeway road to a lay-by on the right hand side of the road. Access is across the road or via the Forestry Commission path near the recycling bins.

SOUTH POORTON

20.69 hectares. Jointly owned with the Grasslands Trust. The strip lynchets around the hidden village of South Poorton provide evidence of how the steeply sloping hillsides were originally farmed. Much remains open grassland & is grazed to maintain the habitat.
Wildlife interest: Range of flora includes dwarf thistle & small scabious on the drier grassy areas & yellow iris & marsh arrowgrass in the boggy ground adjacent to the stream. Mammals include dormouse, harvest mouse & badger. Goldfinch & linnet are seen, with the occasional wheatear passing through in the spring.

South Poorton: lower field and bog area.

Best time to visit: Any time, with late spring & summer probably best.
Access: Limited due to the steep slopes & boggy ground, particularly after heavy rain.
Location: Map ref. SY 513977. Turn off the A356 at the Rampisham masts and head 3 miles south-west or take the road north out of Powerstock for a mile to reach South Poorton. Access to the reserve is from left side of the narrow winding road leading out to the W. of the village (Ridgeback Lane). Small car park on the reserve.

SOVELL DOWN

1.6 hectares. Evidence of ancient ditches & chalk extraction. A Roman road, the Ackling Dyke, connecting Exeter with London, crosses the site. The chalk downland, an oasis in an area of improved grassland & arable fields, is grazed to control scrub invasion, encouraging many typical grass meadow wildflowers.
Wildlife interest: As well as several orchid species,

ABOVE Sovell Down.

BELOW The woodland scene at Stonehill Down.

numbers of typical chalk grassland flowers are found, including clustered bellflower, narrow-leaved sweet briar, rock rose & dwarf sedge. These encourage butterflies such as Adonis blues & marbled whites.

Best time to visit: Early spring for a display of violets & cowslips & into summer for other species.

Access: Difficult due to the uneven ground.

Location: Map ref. ST 992105. Take the A354 Blandford to Salisbury road. Turn right at signpost to Gussages/Horton. After ½ mile turn left to Gussage St. Michael. At junction in village turn right. The reserve is approximately ½ mile along road. Park by water pumping station & take footpath uphill to the reserve.

The wet meadow at Sutton Holms.

STONEHILL DOWN

20 hectares. High on the chalk ridge running west/east across the Isle of Purbeck, this downland reserve has far-reaching views across the Wareham Forest, with Poole Harbour to the east.

Wildlife interest: Common spotted, early purple & bee orchids in early summer. Downland flowers in profusion, including horseshoe vetch & carline thistle. Woodland show of primroses & ramsons. Lulworth skipper & Adonis blue butterflies may be seen.

Best time to visit: Spring & summer.

Access: Several paths cross the reserve, but difficult ground conditions make access limited.

Location: Map ref. SY 925825. Turn off A351 at Springfield Country Hotel & continue straight. Take second left signposted East Creech. Access is at the top of the hill opposite Creech Barrow.

SUTTON HOLMS

0.8 hectares. Traditional pasture with a small pond, wet grassland, oak woodland & hedges.

Wildlife interest: Plants found in the wet areas include ragged robin, meadowsweet, spotted & southern marsh orchid. The meadow has betony amongst the grasses & cow-wheat grows in the woodland. Orange tip butterflies early in the year, followed by marbled whites.

Best time to visit: Spring, as the reserve wakes up.

Access: Before visiting please make prior arrangement with Dorset Wildlife Trust. Very wet ground conditions.

Location: Map ref. SU 058100. Turn south off A354 (Blandford to Salisbury road) onto B3081. Follow road until you reach the B3078 (Cranborne to Wimborne road), turn right. Continue until reaching the B3081, turn left, signposted Heavy Horse Centre. Sutton Holms is 1 mile along on the left just before right hand bend, along a small wooded drive. Parking for 2 cars.

TADNOLL 44.5 hectares & WINFRITH 103 hectares

Unchanged for centuries & still managed using traditional techniques. The dry heath, a carpet of purple in late summer, & wet boggy areas with acid peaty pools are home to many wildlife species, some quite rare. The Tadnoll Brook chalk stream runs through the reserve & is connected to the flood meadows which support a range of

ABOVE Tadnoll Heath

BELOW Winfrith Heath

Orchids at Townsend.

wading birds over the winter months.

Wildlife interest: Birds include hobby, nightjar, woodlark and Dartford warbler. Many interesting dragon & damselflies live in the wetter areas, with silver-studded blue butterflies on the open heaths. Flowers include greater burnet & marsh cinquefoil in the meadows & bog asphodel, heath orchids & sphagnum mosses in the wet areas.

Best time to visit: High summer, but there is likely to be something of interest at any time of the year.

Access: Ground uneven & boggy in places, but several marked trails cross the reserves.

Location: Map ref. Tadnoll SY 791875 & Winfrith SY 809876

Tadnoll – On the A352 take the first left turn after Owermoigne. After the mill on the left continue for approx. 500m. Park on roadside. (New parking area under construction) Tadnoll reserve is on the right opposite a derelict barn.

Winfrith - On the A352 turn off opposite the Red Lion pub. Entrance to Winfrith reserve is just left after the first turn. Park on the roadside.

TOWNSEND

13 hectares. Limestone grassland, rich in wild-flowers & butterflies, & set high above Swanage Bay enjoying splendid views, on the site of old limestone quarries. The ground has settled to form an uneven landscape of mounds & hollows.

Wildlife interest: Spring & summer flowers include early spider orchid, bastard-toadflax, kidney vetch & yellow rattle. Marbled white & common blue butterflies seen, with speckled woods in the scrubby margins. Great green bush crickets, long-winged cone heads & yellow meadow ants are among the insect species found. Slow-worms & adders are occasionally seen, along with badgers, foxes, roe deer.

Best time to visit: Late spring to mid-summer for the show of wildflowers.

Access: Sloping & uneven ground.

Location: Map ref. SZ 024782. Coming into Swanage on the A351, take the first right on the bend. Take the first right after Spar shop then left, then right onto Panorama road. Carry on up the hill, the reserve is on the left hand side. Roadside parking.

The Moors River at Troublefield.

TROUBLEFIELD

6 hectares. Situated in the flood plain of the Moors River, with a mixture of grazed meadows & scrubby woodland. The river margins, with their wide range of water-loving plants, are home for many insects, particularly dragon & damselflies.

Wildlife interest: Flag iris, purple & yellow loosestrife along the river, with a flourish of arrowhead & yellow water lily in late summer. Meadow thistle covers the grazed area & comfrey dominates the north of the reserve where the scarce chaser is among other dragonflies found. Heron, snipe & water rail found & butterflies include small copper, red admiral & peacock.

Best time to visit: Summer for the flowers, butterflies & dragonflies

Access: Often difficult due to the wet ground.

Location: Map ref. SZ 125978. From Hurn post office travel 0.6km up Matchams Lane, turn left down a hidden track. Follow the track for approx. 250m to a parking area. Follow the track to the right of the house for 50m. Enter the reserve through a field gate.

UPTON HEATH

205 hectares. One of the largest surviving areas of Dorset heathland with views across Poole Harbour, Corfe Castle & the Isle of Purbeck. The nature of the terrain reflects its historic use for pottery & brick making.

Wildlife interest: All 6 British reptile species are found on the dry heath. Stonechats and Dartford warblers. The boggy areas support many dragonfly species as well as carnivorous round-leaved sundew & raft spiders.

Best time to visit: Late summer & autumn.

Access: Limited due to difficult ground conditions.

Location: Map ref. SY 989951. Leave the A35, turn down Longmeadow Lane, Creekmoor, until the junction with Beech Bank Avenue. Park at end of Longmeadow Lane.

WEST BEXINGTON

20 hectares. Spectacular coastal views, with a stretch of the Chesil Beach. Mostly reedbed & scrubby wet meadow, attracting a large range of migrant bird species, including the occasional rarity.

Wildlife interest: Resident species include Cetti's warblers & bearded tits, corn buntings & little owls, with grasshopper warblers, snipe & water rails among the visitors. Field voles, woodmice & dormice attract the interest of predatory species. Southern marsh orchid & cuckoo flower in the grassy areas. The shingle beach has sea kale & yellow-horned poppy.

Best time to visit: Any time, but autumn & late winter/early spring are best for the migrant birds.

Access: Although easily reached, walking on the shingle is never easy. Winter storms can cause flooding, restricting access to the remainder of the

Mixed heathers and western gorse on Upton Heath.

reserve.

Location: Map ref. SY 527866. Turn off the B3157 coast road at Swyre, opposite a pub about 7 miles east of Bridport (signposted West Bexington & The Manor Hotel). Follow road for a mile to its end at the public car park & head west along a footpath to the reserve entrance.

The Chesil Beach and marshland at West Bexington, with yellow-horned poppy in the foreground.

Officers of the Trust

Acknowledgements

All the photographs were taken by Tony Bates, except for the following, and the authors are grateful to those listed below for allowing their inclusion:

M. Barber; page 67: M. Blyth; page 75: Stewart Canham; pages 75 (centre right), 76 (top): Kevin Cook; pages 72 (bottom), 74, 75 (centre left), 75 (bottom), 76 (left): Steve Davis; pages 20, 41, 71: Dovecote Press Collection; pages 17, 21, 75 (top): Andy Fale; page 22 (bottom): The Geological Society of London; 44: Bob Gibbons; pages 46 (right), 58: Martin Hazeldine; page 138: Grahame Austin, Kitchenhams Photography; page 68: Stan Shepherd; page 77 (top left): Graham Spencer; page 135: Sarah Williams; pages 109 (centre right), 109 (bottom right), 134.

We would also like to thank Jane Franklin at Dorset Wildlife Trust for further identification of subjects for the book, and the Dorset County Museum for giving us permission to include the photographs on pages 31, 45, 49 and the photograph from the John Jesty collection on page 61.

Index